D0918439

Italian Immigrants in Rural and Small Town America

Italian Immigrants in Rural and Small Town America

Essays from the
Fourteenth Annual Conference
of the American Italian
Historical Association

Held at the Landmark Center
St. Paul, Minnesota
October 30–31, 1981

Edited by Rudolph J. Vecoli
Immigration History Research Center
University of Minnesota

The American Italian
Historical Association
209 Flagg Place
Staten Island, New York
1987

Founded in 1966, the American Italian Historical Association is an interdisciplinary group of scholars and lay people who share an interest in investigating relationships among Italian Americans, Italy and the Americas. Its members encourage the collection, preservation, study and popularization of materials that illuminate the Italian American experience. The Association promotes research through regional and national activities, including the annual conference and the publication of its proceedings.

The publication of this volume has been made possible by grants from the Stella del Nord Chapter of the AIHA and the Settima Vecoli Memorial Fund of the Immigration History Research Center.

Copyediting and design: Linda Watson

Text preparation: Becky Hall and Anne Bjorkquist Ng

Library of Congress Catalog Card Number: 87-72683

ISBN: 0-934675-14-7

ISSN: 0743-474X

Printed in the United States of America

Contents

Mining Towns

Introduction

Rudolph J. Vecoli

Perhaps it was the writings and photographs of Jacob Riis which fixed in our minds the image of "Little Italy." Mulberry Bend with its teeming tenements and congested streets, its raucous peddlers and ragged children, its cacophony of sounds and smells, became the quintessential Italian neighborhood. In the journalism and sociology of the times, Italian immigrants were depicted as inveterate urban dwellers, huddled in their ethnic enclaves, fearful of venturing forth into the "real America." This assumption regarding Italian Americans as big city dwellers has continued to shape Italian American historiography. Scanning the shelves of books published over the past two decades, one is struck by the number of community studies set in big cities: Boston, Philadelphia, Cleveland, Buffalo, Chicago, Toronto, San Francisco, and of course, New York.

That this should have been so was entirely appropriate, and those monographs have greatly enriched our understanding of the Italian immigrant experience. However, we know that this was not the only experience; that the big city did not exhaust the categories of environments in which the Italians lived and worked. We know that many families (like my own) settled in small factory towns, others in mining villages, and not a few on farms in rural America. Certainly they were a minority, but collectively they amounted to a sizable percentage of the total Italian immigration, and numerically to several hundred thousand. More Italian immigrants inhabited small town and rural America than the entire immigration from many countries. It was

curiosity about these "other" experiences which inspired the theme
for the 1981 AIHA conference. We also believed (and believe) that
only by stretching the canvas to include the full panorama of migration and settlement can we begin to encompass the diversity of the
history of Italians in North America.

The essays in this volume appear to fit naturally under three
rubrics. The first of these, "Migration Networks and Settlement Patterns," includes a cluster of articles that address the process of recruitment, movement and distribution. Who left and why, for what
destination, and how did they get there? In his essay, Ryan Rudnicki
traces the spatial dispersion of the Italians in the agricultural and
mining settlements of eleven northeastern and north-central states.
He does so by using the establishment of churches, Roman Catholic
and Protestant, as indicators of the emergence of Italian colonies. A
historical geographer, Rudnicki introduces the issue of information
channels: how did the potential immigrants learn about the "opportunities" that determined their destination? In his case study of one of
the few organized colonization efforts, Alberto Milani tells the story of
the ill-fated Sunny Side Plantation. Through an analysis of ship passenger lists, he determines the composition of the colony and is able
to trace the fate of specific families. Valentine Belfiglio describes the
process of step migration by which Texas recruited its Italians, Sicilians from the sugarcane fields of Louisiana, northern Italians from the
coal mines of Oklahoma. Utilizing family histories, he describes their
successful adaptation to farming in Texas and their assimilation into
the Texan–Anglo-American culture. The role of *padroni* in recruiting and directing the flow of sojourners is well illustrated by John
Potestio's study of the *Grimaldesi*. The Veltri brothers as railroad
labor contractors controlled the movement of their *paesani* for more
than half a century. The resulting Grimaldi colony of Thunder Bay
then generated its own "pull" through chain migration. John Zucchi's *Friulani*, however, were not *contadini*, but artisans, particularly
in the building trades, who had longstanding traditions of temporary
migrations. A prime example of the migration of skills, the *Friulani*
dispersed in small towns and rural communities as well as in big
cities throughout North America. Zucchi observes that this was not
a random emigration, but that each village in Friuli had its chosen
migration targets.

The second rubric, "Small Town Little Italies," groups together those essays which focus upon particular immigrant colonies. Questions of research methodology and sources are of special interest, since the study of the small community has been more often the province of sociologists and anthropologists than of historians. It is particularly fitting that Carla Bianco discusses the research design, research methods, and findings of her classic work, *The Two Rosetos* (1974). Her application of the concept of syncretism, the melding of traditional and new ways, is a suggestive approach to the process of acculturation. Paola Sensi-Isolani combines several research methodologies in her study of tradition and transition in Occidental, a small town in California. The *Lombardi* and *Toscani* there engaged in farming and lumbering; some from the mountain villages of Lucca continued as *carbonari* (charcoal burners). Sensi-Isolani stresses the high degree of isolation and self-sufficiency these Italians enjoyed. Since World War II, however, acculturation has made such rapid inroads that, she concludes, Occidental is no longer Italian. A similar tale told by John Andreozzi involves immigrants predominantly from Abruzzi-Molise who took up farming in western Wisconsin. Andreozzi explains how the Italians gradually acquired land with earnings from railroad work. He describes how the segregation and prejudice which kept the Italians isolated gradually broke down, leading to the eventual dissolution of the community. Duluth, a somewhat larger "small town," harbored several distinct Italian settlements which were set apart both by the diverse origins of the immigrants and by their occupational specializations. Jacqueline Moran describes how these regional differences and antipathies affected the cultural and social life of the Italians. She too identifies World War II as a watershed in the history of Italian ethnicity in Duluth. Farther north along Lake Superior, Antonio Pucci approaches the history of the Italians in Thunder Bay from a different perspective. Pucci stresses the ethnic and class solidarity of the Italian longshoremen in recurring labor disputes. He highlights the primary role of the Italians in the violent strikes, and the harsh measures used by the authorities against the immigrants. Pucci makes the interesting observation that this history of labor militancy is not part of the oral tradition of the community; informants were reluctant to talk about those events.

The third rubric, "Mining Towns," deals with the America experienced by a large segment of the Italian immigrants. The rapid growth of the mining industry in the United States exerted a major "pull" upon the contemporary emigration from Italy. Given the character of the industry, miners and their families lived in camps, locations, and patches, in isolated and desolate parts of the country. Globe, Arizona, was one of many such mining towns scattered throughout the western states. Phylis Martinelli tells of the Italians, mostly Piedmontese, who worked in the copper mines there. Employing anthropological and sociological approaches, she focuses on folk culture and the manner in which it has changed. Due to out-migration, intermarriage, and acculturation, there is little left of the Italian community, yet she concludes that ethnicity persists, albeit in different forms. Paul Sturgul found a similar disintegration of the formal institutions of the Italians on Wisconsin's Gogebic Iron Range, while they still retained a strong group identity. The early settlers were from northern Italy and the Tyrol (then part of Austria), but later southern Italians arrived in significant numbers. Many, especially the northerners, had had previous mining experience in Europe or America. Sturgul describes the active social and cultural life of the Italians, as well as their rapid advancement in business and politics. With the opening of the iron ranges in Minnesota, many miners were recruited from the Upper Peninsula of Michigan as well as Wisconsin. Rudolph Vecoli describes the spirited participation of the Italians in the labor struggles on the Minnesota Iron Range. While he also finds a persisting Italian presence, he emphasizes the syncretism among the various ethnic groups which has produced an "Iron Ranger" identity and culture.

Readers will draw their own conclusions from these essays with respect to the Italian experience in small town and rural America. However, there are several suggestions scattered through these articles regarding the influence of these environments on Italian American ethnicity which warrant explicit statement. Several of the authors observe that these isolated, sparsely populated areas served to insulate the immigrants from the more rapid and traumatic change undergone in the big cities. Free of the constraints of urban ghetto life, they enjoyed a much higher degree of cultural autonomy and economic self-sufficiency. Prejudice and discrimination, although not absent, were encountered less frequently and less intensely. Because of chain migrations, the immigrants tended to share common village origins, dialects, and folk culture, making for a far greater measure of linguistic and cultural maintenance than in the heterogeneous urban Little Italies. The authors agree in viewing World War II as the turning point in the histories of these small communities. Their protective shells, penetrated by the forces of military service, out-migration, intermarriage, and education, quickly crumbled, giving way to assimilation. Why, one is tempted to ask, were the shells so fragile? These observations are not offered as generalizations on the strength of these essays. Yet they will, we hope, serve a heuristic purpose, inspiring others to ask questions about the influence of environment on the diverse experiences of Italian Americans.

The fourteenth annual conference of the AIHA met at the Landmark Center in St. Paul, October 30 and 31, 1981. It was a well-attended, lively meeting with more than thirty papers presented in the course of two days. The full conference program is included at the rear of this volume. In the selection of those essays to be published I had the welcome assistance of a publication committee of the Association which included William D'Antonio, Richard N. Juliani, Salvatore J. LaGumina, and the late Leonard W. Moss. However, the final determination was made by the editor.

The conference program was distinguished by the wide range of topics covered by the presentations. Geographically, it had a North American scope. One of the gratifying features of the conference was the joint session with the Canadian Italian Historical Association. The contributions of our Canadian colleagues are well represented in this volume. While, appropriately enough, the upper Midwest did receive particular attention, the paper topics extended to many different parts of the United States. They also embodied a diversity of approaches, reflecting the multidisciplinary character of the AIHA membership itself. We hope to have captured some of the stimulating variety in the following pages.

We would like to express our appreciation to all those persons who helped to make the conference a success. In addition to those who presented papers, chaired sessions, or commented, there were many who contributed time and effort to the planning and staging of the conference itself. While space does not permit the listing of the various committees, I wish to acknowledge in particular the enthusiastic support and work of the members of the Stella del Nord Chapter of the AIHA and of the staff of the Immigration History Research Center.

We also gladly recognize the following organizations whose financial contributions made the conference possible: Stella del Nord Chapter, AIHA; Columbus Memorial Association; Italian American Club of Duluth and Women's Auxiliary; St. Paul UNICO Chapter; Italian American Progressive Club of Hibbing; Minnesota Historical Society; and Jeno's Inc.

Finally I wish to express my gratitude to Linda Watson for her indispensable assistance in seeing this manuscript through the editorial process and to Becky Hall and Anne Bjorkquist Ng for the preparation of the manuscript for the printer.

Migration
Networks
and
Settlement
Patterns

Patterns of Italian Immigrant Settlement

Ryan Rudnicki

This paper derives from a larger study whose objective was to recon-
struct the evolution of Italian immigrant population concentrations
in eleven northeastern and north-central states where most Italians
settled.[1] That study focused on the fifty-year period between 1880
and 1930, a period of substantial Italian immigration to the United
States. Between those years the proportion of Italians in America who
lived in the eleven states increased from 60 percent to 86 percent.

Roman Catholic parishes and missions identified in diocesan records
as being for Italians and Italian Protestant (e.g., Presbyterian)
churches were used as indicators of Italian settlements. The presence
of a church was usually a sign that the Italian settlement was relatively large, concentrated, and permanent. The study identified 431
Italian churches organized between 1880 and 1930 in 281 locations
within the eleven-state study area. Although conclusions about the
distribution of Italians presented here are based on the number of
churches and not on the number of people, the words "church" and

---

[1] Ryan Rudnicki, "Peopling Industrial America: Formation of Italian and Polish
Settlements in the Manufacturing Heartland of the United States, 1880–1930"
(Ph.D. diss., Pennsylvania State University, 1979). The eleven-state study area
comprised Massachusetts, Connecticut, Rhode Island, New Jersey, New York,
Pennsylvania, Ohio, Michigan, Indiana, Illinois, and Wisconsin.

"settlement" will be used interchangeably.

The places settled by Italians fell into four broad categories: principal cities; small- to medium-sized manufacturing cities; mining towns; and agricultural villages. This paper describes the geographical patterns and information processes related to the settlement of agricultural villages and mining towns.

Settlement in Villages and Mining Towns

Relatively few Italians settled in agricultural villages and mining towns. The number of Italians in principal cities such as New York, Philadelphia, and Chicago far outweighed the number found in other location types. Rather consistently between 1900 and 1930, 15 percent to 20 percent of all Italian churches were found in agricultural villages and mining towns, with the clear majority in the latter category (Fig. 1). The number of churches in the two categories grew as the number of Italians in the study area increased:

Italian Churches	1880	1890	1900	1910	1920	1930
Agricultural Villages	1	3	4	11	13	15
Mining Towns	0	4	12	36	52	55

The rate of increase fell between 1920 and 1930 because of immigration restrictions passed by Congress in the 1920s. The effect of the legislation was to drastically reduce the immigration of Italians and other southern and eastern Europeans.

Italian rural settlement has a long tradition in the United States. The first rural Italian settlement within the eleven-state study area was established at Genoa, Wisconsin, in the 1860s.[2] Here in the hilly uplands of Vernon County, east of the Mississippi River, a group of Italians from Lombardy and Piedmont decided to settle in an area whose topography reminded them of their native Italy.[3]

The number of Italian agricultural settlements grew slowly. Between 1880 and 1890 two Italian agricultural colonies were established

---

[2] Other early agricultural settlements were located in the South and West. See Andrew Rolle, *The Immigrant Upraised* (Norman, Okla., 1968); and Jean Scarpaci, "Immigrants in the New South: Italians in Louisiana's Sugar Parishes, 1880–1910" in Francesco Cordasco, ed., *Studies in Italian American Social History* (Totowa, N.J., 1975).

[3] Alexander E. Cance, "Piedmontese on the Mississippi," *Survey* 26 (2 September 1911): 779–85.

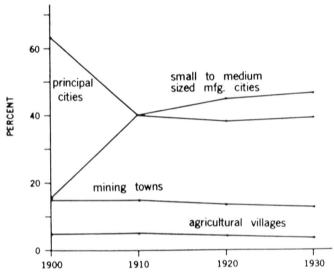

Figure 1. Percentage of Italian churches by settlement category, 1900–1930.

in southern New Jersey. In the following decade only one new farming village was established, at Cumberland, Wisconsin. At the end of the nineteenth century only four agricultural settlements dotted the landscape of the eleven states. This number more than doubled during the first decade of the twentieth century, bringing the total to eleven in 1910. The new settlements emerged in two distinct areas, one old and one new. In southern New Jersey, the old agricultural area, Italian rural settlers increased and four additional missions and parishes were established. The new area of agricultural settlement was in upstate New York between Buffalo and Rochester; three churches were organized in that region. After that expansion the number of Italian agricultural settlements increased very slowly between 1910 and 1930. Two of the four new churches set up during the period were in a new region, eastern Long Island. The other two churches were organized in the upstate New York agricultural settlement area. By 1930 Italians had established only fifteen churches, a mere 4 percent of the total number in the United States, in agricultural villages (Fig. 2).

The first mining community churches were established in the 1880s. Three were in Pennsylvania's anthracite coal region, at Carbondale, Hazleton, and Lattimer. The fourth church was established at Iron Mountain, Michigan, in the Menominee Range along the Michigan-Wisconsin border. During the 1890s, eight new Italian churches were founded in mining towns. Three were in northeastern Pennsylvania's anthracite region. By 1900, this region was defined by a cluster of settlements. A fourth colony emerged at Vulcan in the Menominee Range iron region of Michigan's Upper Peninsula, an area that continued to attract Italians. The remaining four new Italian mining colonies established during the 1890s represented new kinds of resource extraction. In western Pennsylvania and southern Illinois, the first Italian colonies were established in bituminous coal fields. One colony was located at Walston, Pennsylvania, in the great Punxsutawney coke region. Italians here worked not only as miners but also as coke drawers and coke laborers. Another bituminous coal colony was organized at Herrin, Illinois. On Michigan's Keweenaw Peninsula, Italians established a parish in the copper mining town of Calumet. A variant of the mining town colony emerged at Roseto, Pennsylvania, where Italians worked in slate quarries.

Between 1880 and 1900 the number of Italian churches in mining towns more than doubled. Between 1900 and 1910, the number of churches tripled, from 12 to 36. These churches were established in the same areas that had attracted Italians in previous decades. Most noticeable was the blossoming of churches in Pennsylvania's bituminous region. Churches were also formed in Pennsylvania's anthracite region, and a few were established in the bituminous coal towns of Illinois, including Toluca, Coal City, and Benld. The Keweenaw copper region added a church at Franklin Mine. The nearby iron mining areas in the Gogebic and Menominee ranges added two Italian churches as well, including one at Iron River. An unusual kind of mining settlement was established at Grand Rapids, Michigan, in 1908. Italians worked in the gypsum mines southwest of the city. At Johnston, Rhode Island, granite quarries, and the Italians employed there, were the reason an Italian church was organized.

The number of Italian churches in mining communities increased significantly, though at a slower rate, between 1910 and 1920, from 36 to 52. During the twenties the establishment of new mining set-

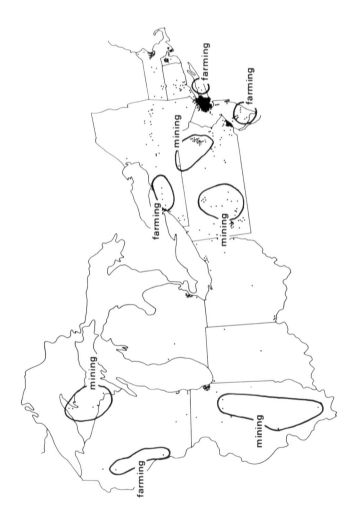

Figure 2. Italian churches in farming and mining areas to 1930.

tlements slowed further; only three new churches were formed, the lowest ten-year total since 1880. In 1930, the 55 Italian mining town churches accounted for a small, but noticeable, 14 percent of all Italian churches in the eleven states under study (Fig. 2).

Information Channels

Italian immigrants did not simply appear at a farming or mining site by chance and begin working and building homes. Immigrant laborers responded to information about existing settlement and employment opportunities. By what channels did this information travel?

Perhaps the best place to begin is with the research of Charlotte Erickson.[4] She identified five different kinds of information channels by which Europeans learned about economic opportunities in the United States: recruitment in Europe by agents of steamship companies and American industries; company recruiters at ports of arrival; private labor agencies (including the *padroni* among Italians); public labor agencies; and personal information in the form of letters from American immigrant colonies to European villages.

When applied to the Italian experience Erickson's list is useful, but it does not adequately describe the information channels that guided immigrants to potential agricultural and mining town sites. First, an information channel must be added—the real estate agent; second, an established channel must be expanded—personal information; third, the various channels should be seen as working together.

Real estate agents in the United States advertised to inform Italians of settlement opportunities. Two examples of the real estate agent's role follow. In the southern New Jersey communities of Hammonton and East Vineland, the real estate developer was Charles K. Landis, a Philadelphia lawyer and banker who had visions of a southern New Jersey settled by sturdy agriculturalists who would make the region bloom and establish a great city in the wilderness. Landis purchased 32,000 acres and established the town of Vineland in 1861. To discourage speculation, he sold only small lots of 5, 10, or 15 acres. He and his salesmen advertised heavily in New York among native Americans and the foreign born. His advertisements attracted the attention of Secchi di Casale, editor of *L'Eco d'Italia* in New York City. The two

---

[4] Charlotte Erickson, *American Industry and the European Immigrant, 1860–1885* (Cambridge, Mass., 1957).

men worked out favorable financing terms that were within the means
of southern Italian immigrants.[5] In Cumberland, Wisconsin, real estate agents also spurred settlement by Italian immigrants. There, real
estate speculators convinced some Italian railroad construction workers in the area that the region was good for farming. Because the price
was low, a number of Italians bought land and established a farming
community.[6]

What Erickson called the personal information channel, or letters
from America, must be expanded to fit the Italian experience. Among
Italians, some letters never had to leave America to effectively steer
Italians to potential settlement sites. A large pool of unemployed or
partially employed Italians already in the United States responded to
personal information channels within this country. Letters about job
opportunities were sent to relatives who lived in other parts of the
country. Information was also passed by word of mouth, through immigrant grocers, saloon keepers, boardinghouse owners, and priests.
Finally, advertisements that appeared in newspapers around the country played a role in spreading the word about jobs among Italian
immigrants.

Examples of these forms of the personal information channel are
numerous. Certain Italians in Buffalo had relatives in Pennsylvania
coal towns with whom they corresponded. When Italians lost their
jobs in Buffalo, they left to join relatives in Pennsylvania who told
them that mine operators were hiring. Conversely, when miners struck
for higher wages and better working conditions in the Pennsylvania
mines, a number of Italians moved back to Buffalo where they once
again found work.[7] Perhaps the same pattern was followed in the iron
mines of Upper Michigan. A number of those Italians were recruited
from Chicago. Again, some family members and friends stayed in
Chicago while others moved north. Presumably the two groups advised each other of the changing economic climate of their respective

---

[5] Robert F. Foerster, *The Italian Emigration of Our Times* (Cambridge, Mass.,
1919), p. 367. Altruistic efforts to move immigrants out of the city and into a rural
environment perceived as more healthful were popular during the 1880s. See, for
example, Joseph Brandes, *Immigrants to Freedom: Jewish Communities in Rural
New Jersey Since 1882* (Philadelphia, 1971).

[6] Foerster, *Italian Emigration*, p. 366; Luciano J. Iorizzo and Salvatore Mondello,
The Italian Americans (New York, 1971), p. 121.

[7] Virginia Yans-McLaughlin, *Family and Community* (Ithaca, N.Y., 1977), p.
77.

settlement choices and moved when necessary.[8]

A more formal variant of this information channel consisted of newspaper ads for labor. For example, bituminous coal operators in Illinois very likely encouraged anthracite miners to move westward by advertising for labor in Pennsylvania anthracite region newspapers.[9] At the moment, however, the impact of this information channel on Italians is speculation. More research is clearly needed.

Personal contact was an important channel of information. Italian saloon keepers, grocers, and boardinghouse operators were approached by local mine operators who needed labor. Migrant Italians (often railroad construction laborers) learned about jobs from the owners of these businesses. This channel accounted for the presence of some early Italian settlers in the anthracite mining town of Carbondale and the bituminous coal town of Annedale, Pennsylvania.[10]

The third change to Erickson's schema involves interaction of the information channels. Two or more information channels frequently operated either simultaneously or sequentially to steer Italian immigrants to specific settlement sites. The most common occurrence involved two information channels; one brought Italians into an area, the other helped to make them permanent settlers in the region. In upstate New York, for example, Italians were hired at canneries and farms during the harvest season through the efforts of *padroni* who recruited workers from nearby cities, especially Buffalo. Once in the agricultural region, some Italians learned about farmland that was for sale and settled in the area. Other Italians came into this agricultural region as day laborers on railroad projects and on the expansion of the Erie Barge Canal. Most likely, immigrants obtained these jobs through *padroni*. Subsequently, they learned of available farmland near their construction work and purchased it. The Italian colonies at Farnham, Fredonia, Falconer, Silver Creek, Sheridan, Brant, and Albion, New York, trace their roots, at least in part, to the operation of the multifaceted information process.[11]

---

[8] Monsignor David Spelgatti, interview with author, Ishpeming, Mich., 1 November 1978.

[9] Harold Aurand, "The Anthracite Mine Workers, 1869–1897: A Functional Approach to Labor History" (Ph.D. diss., Pennsylvania State University, 1969), p. 115.

[10] *Our Lady of Mt. Carmel Church, 75th Anniversary* (Carbondale, Pa., 1975), p. 3; G. Tiche, interview with author, Boyers, Pa., 11 March 1975.

[11] Virginia Yans-McLaughlin, "A Flexible Tradition: South Italian Immigrants

Conclusion

This paper has just begun to explore the role of information channels in the historical geography of Italian immigrants. The nature of information channels remains to be identified for each Italian colony. Which channel was most important in guiding the first Italians to a settlement site? Did the importance of certain channels vary among Italians from different regions of Italy? What impact did newspaper advertisements have in bringing Italians to specific locales? To what extent did Italians respond to encouraging letters from friends and relatives in other parts of the United States? For that matter, how much interaction was there among the various Italian colonies?

Although information channels were important, they are just one of several factors that produced the particular spatial distribution that characterized Italian agricultural and mining settlements. From a geographical perspective, for example, it is also important to know how Italians perceived the physical environment of the northern states. Did that perception play a role in producing such a small number of Italian agricultural settlements?

Finally, only when we have a complete picture of the distribution of Italian communities, not just in agricultural and mining areas but also in principal cities and small- to medium-sized manufacturing towns, can we produce truly representative studies of Italian life in various places, or kinds of places, in America. The fragmented picture that now exists limits the usefulness of individual community studies. How representative of the Italian settlement history are these individual studies? When we know the answer to that question, we will be well on our way to answering the larger question of the impact of Italian immigrants on the settlement and growth of America.

Confront a New Work Experience," *Journal of Social History*, Summer 1974, p. 434; Iorizzo and Mondello, *Italian Americans*, pp. 123, 125, 126.

Marchigiani and Veneti on Sunny Side Plantation

Ernesto Milani

The pattern of Italian immigration to the south-central United States[1] during the period of mass migration, 1880–1914, is characteristic of a general lack of interest shown by immigrants toward this region. In the years prior to 1880, fearing the possible disturbance that new-comers might create in its way of life, the South had a closed-gate policy. Later, the East was the main attraction for immigrants. In addition, the predominantly black population of certain areas posed a race problem that European immigrants preferred not to confront upon their arrival. Further, it was thought that the conservative and arrogant attitude of the Southern ruling class had not changed much after the Civil War, and in fact white immigrants who engaged in manual labor that also was performed by blacks were regarded as belonging to an inferior race. Another commonplace was the notion that cotton, an unknown crop in Europe, was the only crop cultivated in the South and grew in marshy areas where the hot summer temper-

---

[1] Kentucky, Tennessee, Alabama, Mississippi, Louisiana, Oklahoma, Texas, and Arkansas.

atures were unbearable and malaria-related diseases were rampant.[2]

No wonder, then, that of the massive flow of Italian immigrants to the United States, which averaged 211,294 persons a year between 1901 and 1908, only a few—2,172 per year—chose to settle in the south-central states. Louisiana and Texas were the most popular destinations; Louisiana accepted 60.7 percent of these immigrants, Texas 9.7 percent; the remainder were scattered among the other states.

In Louisiana Italians found work in the sugar plantations, in various agricultural settlements such as Independence, and also in the port city of New Orleans, where the Italian community was quite prominent in spite of the infamous lynchings of Italians that occurred in 1891.[3]

During the same 1901–1908 period, Arkansas attracted an average of only 45 Italian immigrants per year, despite a strange apex in 1907, when 196 people went there. As of 1 June 1900, the number of Arkansans born in Italy numbered only 576, or 2.1 percent of the total Italian population residing in the south-central states. As of 30 June 1908 the Italian-born population was estimated at 1,360 individuals, who represented a mere 2 percent of the 69,543 Italian-born residents of the south-central states. That in turn was only 4 percent of the Italian-born population of the entire United States.[4] Despite the paucity of Italian immigrants in the south-central states and in Arkansas in particular, there is an interesting episode in Italian American history which focuses on Sunny Side Plantation, Arkansas.

The Italians of Arkansas settled primarily in three locations: 1) Little Rock, where they numbered about a hundred and were engaged in small business, fruit vending, and barbering; 2) Tontitown, which was located a few miles north of Springdale on the northwestern side of the state, very near the Oklahoma border; and 3) Sunny Side Plantation, which was situated in the southeastern part of the

---

[2] Walter F. Fleming, "Immigration to the Southern States," *Political Science Quarterly* 20 (June 1905): 276–97.

[3] See Jean A. Scarpaci, *Italian Immigrants in Louisiana's Sugar Parishes: Recruitment, Labor Conditions and Community Relations, 1880–1910* (New York, 1981).

[4] Ministero degli Affari Esteri, Commissariato per l'Emigrazione, *Emigrazione e colonie: Raccolta di rapporti consolari*, vol. 3, *America* (Rome, 1909). The article on the Italian population in America is a report from the Italian embassy in Washington, "Gli Stati Uniti e l'immigrazione italiana, da un rapporto della regia ambasciata in Washington," pp. 44–69.

state between Lake Chicot and the Mississippi River.[5]

Sunny Side, a cotton plantation, was a grand agricultural scheme that lured almost a thousand Italians to rural Arkansas near the turn of the century. What the immigrants found there was not the better life they were seeking, but a bewildering system of agriculture in a harsh climate. Today nothing remains of Sunny Side except a mound on the northern tip of Lake Chicot where, in a fenced-in cemetery, only a few tombstones have survived.

John C. Calhoun, grandson of the famous American statesman, is the first person linked to the Sunny Side experiment. He bought the old Florence Plantation located on the Mississippi riverfront on the southern part of Lake Chicot. This enterprise was designed to redevelop the area after the Civil War. Since this initial purchase proved successful, he conceived the idea of buying more plantations in order to unite them as a single property. The plantations around Lake Chicot suited his plan. He gradually obtained the option to buy most of these plantations and also succeeded in convincing some wealthy friends to join him in this unusual enterprise. Austin Corbin, a banker and owner of the Long Island Railway, was very interested. Calhoun raised the money needed, and soon after his return from New York managed to acquire most of the plantations around Lake Chicot.[6]

As soon as the legal aspects of the various transactions were defined, the Sunny Side Company was incorporated on 9 April 1887 under the laws of the state of Connecticut, with Austin Corbin appointed as president.[7] Sunny Side thus became one large plantation, consisting of about 10,000 acres which had long been neglected and were in need of restoration. The new company sold bonds worth more than half a million dollars; this money was to improve the plantation. A small railroad was built to carry the cotton crops to the Sunny Side landing and speed them to the Greenville market across the Mississippi. Sunny Side and Lake Village, on the southern tip of Lake Chicot, were then

---

[5] Ministero degli Affari Esteri, *America*, "Gli Italiani nel distretto consolare di Nuova Orleans, da un rapporto del cav. Giacomo Fara Forni con aggiunte del cav. Luigi Villari, r. addetto consolare per l'emigrazione," p. 212; *Bollettino dell'emigrazione* no. 8 (Rome, 1905), pp. 34–35.

[6] Ed Trice, "Shadows over Sunnyside," *Chicot Spectator*, 26 June 1936, p. 14.

[7] W.J. Lemke, *The Story of Tontitown, Arkansas* (Fayetteville, Ark., 1963). The book includes a reproduction of the contract signed by the Italian immigrants with the Sunny Side Company and bears the incorporation date.

connected by regular boat service. Eventually the plantation's wooden houses, cribs, and warehouses were repaired or rebuilt. The company established its headquarters near the Mississippi River landing with a company store nearby to provide necessities for the tenants and a gin to process the cotton before shipping. The company was ready for a more profitable operation, but almost immediately faced an unforeseen labor shortage. The black tenants, more afraid of a new owner from the North than of their former landlords, preferred to follow the latter, leaving half the land and houses unattended.

At a time when the South was debating about replacing black labor with European immigrants—especially unskilled ones such as the Italians who were flocking to New York by the thousands—it was easy for Corbin to propose a solution.[8] Austin Corbin was a well-known entrepreneur. Born on 11 July 1827 in Newport, New Hampshire, he became famous as a banker in Iowa. Eventually his success led him back East, where he set up financial institutions in New York, one of which was Austin Corbin and Company. He also was involved in the railroad business, and his interest in mass transportation helped him to reorganize the Long Island Railway System. His goals were high; he even had plans for an underground rail system throughout New York and a steamship harbor on Long Island to shorten the Atlantic crossing. However, no mention is made in biographies of his interest in the South and his role in the Sunny Side Company. Corbin is described in various biographies as an energetic person, self-reliant, independent, and a natural leader. He is not described as a philanthropist, though use of that term is standard in such works.[9]

Corbin, determined to solve the manpower shortage on Sunny Side Plantation, turned for help to the newly established Italian Bureau of Labor of New York. The office on Ellis Island had been set up in 1894 by Baron Saverio Fava, a former diplomat of the Bourbon kingdom, removed from his post by Garibaldi and later readmitted to the diplomatic corps in secondary posts. He had been the Italian ambassador to Washington, at that time not a prestigious posting, since 1881.[10] Baron Fava gave control of the Bureau of Labor to his rela-

---

[8] Robert L. Brandfon, "The End of Immigration to the Cotton Fields," *Mississippi Valley Historical Review*, March 1964, pp. 591–611; Alfred Holt Stone, *Studies in the American Race Problem* (New York, 1908).

[9] *The National Cyclopedia of American Biography*, 1944 ed.; *Dictionary of American Biography*, 1958 ed.; *Who Was Who in America*, 1963 ed.

[10] Alfredo Canavero, "Stampa e opinione pubblica italiana di fronte alla guerra

tive, Alessandro Oldrini. Both Fava and Oldrini had been accused of wrongdoing by a strange character, Celso Caesar Moreno, who called them ruffians and accomplices of the notorious *padroni*.[11] Although Moreno was indicted for this, the truth of his accusations has not yet been fully ascertained.[12] Capital to support the Bureau came from several sources, including the Italian *prominenti* and the Italian government. However, a certain offer of $1,200 was rejected. The donor was Austin Corbin.[13]

Because of his need for labor for Sunny Side, Corbin got in touch with Oldrini and Fava once more. He explained his desire to employ Italians on his plantation. The proposal fit the requirements of the Italian officials, who saw the diversion of Italians to more "natural" rural activities as an alternative to the crowded conditions of the Eastern cities. Corbin, according to Fava, was a philanthropist, and his description of Sunny Side sounded like utopia. However, Fava did not actually go to Sunny Side. Instead, he sent a casual visitor from Rome, Emanuele Ruspoli, whom he refers to as an agriculturalist, but who was evidently a landowner and politician.[14]

Ruspoli's report was very favorable. The same government that had not accepted the money Corbin offered for the Italian Labor Bureau of New York fully concurred in endorsing a contract-labor deal contrary to the Foran Act of 1885, which not only prohibited the importation of foreigners under contract or agreement to perform labor in the United States, but also prohibited prepayment of transportation for immigrants and voided labor contracts issued before immigration. In the meantime, Baron Fava managed to obtain the approval of the American government to begin the scheme.[15]

Corbin met with Ruspoli, and the new project—the Sunny Side

---

ispano-americana del 1898," in G. Spini et al., *Italia e America dal Settecento all'età dell'imperialismo* (Lama Umbro, 1976); De Gubernatis, *Dizionari biografici* (Rome, 1895).

[11] Celso Caesar Moreno, *History of a Great Wrong: Italian Slavery in America* (New York, 1896).

[12] Francesca Loverci, "Il primo ambasciatore italiano a Washington: Saverio Fava," *Clio*, July-September 1977, pp. 239–76.

[13] Saverio Fava, "Le colonie agricole italiane nell'America del Nord," *Nuova Antologia*, 1 October 1904, pp. 462–68.

[14] Ibid.; letter from Emanuele Ruspoli to Bishop Scalabrini, 31 January 1895, Centro Studi Emigrazione Roma Historical Archives, Rome; *Enciclopedia Italiana Treccani*, 1936 ed., s.v. "Emanuele Ruspoli."

[15] Fava, "Le colonie agricole," pp. 466–67.

Company— was set up. Ruspoli, as the Italian representative, was to recruit 100 families a year for five years and send them to Sunny Side. The contract was clear. The would-be cotton growers were obligated to the company for twenty-two years in order to become owners of the land they were going to cultivate. The terms of purchase were predicated on 5 percent annual interest and a price of $160 an acre, when the average market price ranged from $40 to $50 an acre, or as low as $3 an acre for untilled land. Sunny Side land could be rented for $5 to $7 an acre, depending on location and the fertility of the soil. Although still exorbitant, rent was more acceptable to the immigrants because they could better control their expenses and take advantage of every lump of soil. The terms dictated by the company did not seem harsh on paper, but one may wonder how many colonists really understood what they were going to grow, where they were going to settle, and all the complications of this new mode of farming.[16]

They probably could not have realized that the company would practically control the cotton business, and therefore their lives, because it operated the gin, the packing house, and the railroad through the plantation. The company also ran the only store in the area, thus making the entire operation a profitable closed process for the company. This was not mentioned in the contract, although Article 7 explained part of it.[17]

Ruspoli was working hard to fulfill the Italian part of Corbin's design and ensure that a flow of people reached the Mississippi shores. On his return to Rome from New York Ruspoli wrote a letter to Bishop Scalabrini, founder of the religious order that ministered to the Italian immigrants:

> Mi sono inteso con un grande capitalista mio amico, Mr. Corbin, per impiantare una colonia agricola in una grande proprietà e formarvi un paese italiano che sia esempio di attività e ben essere.[18]

Ruspoli added that he had visited the plantation on behalf of the Italian embassy and praised the good climate and the restoration

---

[16] Lemke, *Tontitown*.

[17] Ibid. The Sunny Side Company, if requested, would have bought the cotton at the New Orleans Stock Exchange price minus the tariffs and transportation expenses from Sunny Side to New Orleans, or no more than $1 per bale of cotton.

[18] Ruspoli to Scalabrini, 31 January 1895: "I have made an agreement with a great capitalist friend of mine, Mr. Corbin, to establish a rural colony on a large property and set up an Italian village that may be an example of well-being."

work he found. He requested that a priest be sent to Sunny Side, in particular one of the missionaries already present in New York. Father Pietro Bandini was assigned to the new settlement. Ruspoli asked Scalabrini to notify the priests under his jurisdiction to gather families for the first expedition.

It did not take long to organize the first departure. At that time, conditions favored immigration to the United States. The economies of Argentina and Brazil could no longer accept masses of people; rapidly growing American industry required labor and the importation of Chinese workers was banned. The steamship lines were ready to shift their routes to tap this potentially rich market, and their agents scoured rural areas of Italy looking for passengers. The exodus from the rural villages of Veneto helped the search, which was extended to the Marches region where the Bishop of Senigallia was actively recruiting immigrants.[19]

The first contingent of settlers formed rapidly. Recoaro, Valle dei Signori (now Valli del Pasubio), and Staro, all in the province of Vicenza, gave their share. Others came from Senigallia in the province of Ancona, from the little hamlets of Montemarciano, Ostra, Chiaravalle, and most of all Montignano. A few scattered families came from the province of Rieti.[20]

It was not hard to enroll people, because the recruiters knew where the areas of heavy emigration were. The emigrants signed their contracts and prepared to leave with their belongings, knowing they probably would never return. The group from Recoaro left from the railway station of Tavernelle, traveling to Milan and then Genoa, where they joined others coming from Senigallia and the Alto Lazio. Ruspoli had done his job well. His letter to Scalabrini made it seem that he was part of the venture, and indeed he did his best to ensure the success of the expedition. The first group of prospective cotton growers left in the fall of 1895, as planned by Ruspoli. Their ship, the *Chateau Yquem*, left the port of Genoa on 8 November 1895 and called at New Orleans on 22 November. The immigrants reached the Sunny Side landing on 4 December, after four days of navigation up

---

[19] Emilio Franzina, *La grande emigrazione: L'esodo dei rurali dal Veneto durante il secolo XIX* (Venice, 1976).

[20] Bob Edmisten, "Tontitown Old-Timers Cherish Italian Language," *Springdale News*, 14 August 1980, p. 11A.

the Mississippi River in an Anchor Line boat owned by Corbin.[21]

According to the passenger manifest signed by the French master, Jules Chabot, there were 562 people on board, and Chabot in fact paid $562 landing tax, or $1 per passenger, as required by existing laws. However, the passenger list shows only 456 names (6 are not recorded and the count skips from 280 to 381; most probably those 106 names were omitted by mistake.) The list contains frequent anglicizations and gallicisms; most names are either misspelled or first and family names are transposed. The passenger list is valuable for understanding the composition of the first group of settlers. There were seventy-three families, of which sixty-seven were headed by husband and wife, two by husband only, and four by wife only. The average age of male heads of family was thirty-nine, of wives, thirty-five. Louis and Louise Tomiello were the oldest couple at seventy-one and seventy-three, respectively. Dominick and Antonia Zulpo were the youngest couple; both were twenty-six.

Most of the people on the passenger list were traveling in families. The total number of people in family groups was 433; there were only 21 persons traveling alone. There were 238 children—more than half the 456 passengers named on the manifest. One child was born at sea; 4 children died during the voyage. The average number of children per family was slightly over 3.

The second ship bound for America and Sunny Side Plantation, the *Kaiser Wilhelm der Grosse*, left Genoa on 14 December 1896. This ship called at New York harbor on 29 December.[22] From there the immigrants continued their journey by rail and reached Sunny Side on 2 January 1897. The *Kaiser Wilhelm's* passenger list was very accurate, and, unlike the *Chateau Yquem's* list, reported the relationships among the passengers. The *Kaiser Wilhelm* had three classes, while the *Chateau Yquem* had only steerage.

Kaiser Wilhelm	*Adults*	*Children*	*Infants*	*Total*
First Cabin	27	3	0	30
Second Cabin	11	3	1	15
Steerage	341	109	19	469
Total	379	115	20	514

---

[21] Passenger Arrival Records, National Archives, Washington, D.C., M259 R81.

[22] Passenger Arrival Records, National Archives, Washington, D.C., M237 R0669.

One page of the passenger manifest (30 names) is obviously missing; it is undoubtedly the one that lists the Zulpo family. Guglielmina Zulpo (named after the ship), born at sea on 21 December 1896, was recorded on the last page but her family does not appear anywhere else.

The total number of passengers who listed Arkansas as their destination was 376. Among the would-be cotton growers were sixty-six families. The average age of male heads of family was thirty-nine, of wives, thirty-four. Angelo and Maria Piazza were the oldest couple at sixty-nine and sixty-five, respectively. Pietro and Maria Gregandi were the youngest couple; both were twenty-one years old. There were 126 children under twelve, and 35 young people over twelve; 64 passengers were members of extended families and 19 traveled alone.

The chain migration had already started. This second ship included many travelers who were joining relatives already at Sunny Side. It is important to stress that this migration was contrary to the norm for that time, since it was composed of family groups. The departure of complete families explains the lack of information obtainable in some cases in the villages of origin.[23] On the *Kaiser Wilhelm*, for example, the extended-family members composed almost 20 percent of the total, and some of them were quite old. In fact, sixteen passengers, or more than 4 percent, were over sixty years of age.

When the second group of immigrants arrived at Sunny Side, conditions on the plantation had already deteriorated. Although everything seemed in order at the beginning, and the presence of Father Pietro Bandini provided both confidence and material help, very soon the climate proved unbearable and the problems of this new type of agriculture almost insurmountable. Fevers completely unknown to the Italians created a panic that was difficult to dispel. They were advised to take precautions, such as putting nets on the windows, avoiding walking barefoot in the morning and evening dew, and being careful of the source of their drinking water. Still, people continued to die of fever. In addition, the sudden death of Austin Corbin when the colony

---

[23] Personal visits to Recoaro and Chiaravalle have revealed that the municipal archives were lost during World War II. Monsignor Polverari of the Diocese of Senigallia has informed me that the file on Father Garrone, who went to Sunny Side in 1904, and the files on emigration are missing from the library. Other investigations in private homes secured only marginal material and a 1911 photo of the Pozza family of Recoaro taken in Tontitown.

was not yet completely organized contributed to the problems.[24] Finally, the price of cotton had dropped. Corbin's heirs, who could not cope with managing the cotton plantation, leased the property to O.B. Crittenden & Company of Greenville, Mississippi. The company, under the leadership of O.B. Crittenden, a prominent Southern planter, was familiar with all aspects of cotton plantations.[25]

All reports concur that two major difficulties hampered the progress of the colony—fear of disease and the economic stress of learning new farming techniques in the South. Because of these problems, the colony split in the spring of 1898. Some people followed Father Bandini and set out for the Ozarks, where they founded Tontitown. Another group headed by A.M. Piazza went farther north and established Knobview (now Rosati) in Missouri.[26] Those who remained were determined to survive and immediately met the conditions imposed by the new managers, businessmen who had no utopian dreams. Their first edict, issued on 1 February 1898, declared that too many benefits had been given the colonists and that these would be eliminated. The mules, the doctor, the priest, the teacher, the gardener, the heating for the church, the railroad, and the filter for the water all had a price that the colonists must now pay.[27]

Most of those who remained were from the same province, Ancona, which made things a little easier. Those who stayed believed that things would improve with hard work, persistence, and a bit of good luck. After all, the soil was extremely fertile and after some time cotton farming would become familiar. In fact, 1898 proved to be a good year for cotton, and it encouraged the colonists to stay. Of course, the problems of mosquitoes, poor wells and drainage systems, and exploitation by the planters remained, but there was faith that after so many deaths, after so much sorrow, things would improve.

Data from the census of 1900 reveal what happened to Sunny Side

---

[24] Corbin died from injuries received in a carriage accident in Newport, New Hampshire, on 4 June 1896. *The National Cyclopedia of American Biography*.

[25] U.S. Immigration Commission, *Reports of the Immigration Commission*, vol. 21, *Immigrants in Industries: Pt. 24, Recent Immigrants in Agriculture*, 61st Cong., 2d sess., S. Doc. no. 633 (Washington, D.C., 1911), pp. 319–37.

[26] Lemke, *Tontitown*; Giovanni Schiavo, *The Italians in Missouri* (New York, 1929), pp. 152–54; Rev. P. Pietro Bandini, "Origine della colonia di Tontitown, nell'Arkansas," *Bollettino dell'emigrazione* no. 1 (Rome, 1903), pp. 61–62.

[27] "Ai Coloni Italiani di Sunny Side, Ark.," notice from the Sunny Side Co. to the Sunny Side colonists, 1 February 1898, E.R. Milani personal papers.

Plantation settlers between January 1897 and June 1900. According to the census, no new arrivals were recorded between 1897 and 1900. Most names listed in the census also were on either the *Chateau Yquem* or *Kaiser Wilhelm* passenger list; discrepancies most likely are due to the inaccuracy of the passenger lists.[28] Altogether, 175 people—only 18 percent of the 938 who had come to Sunny Side on the *Kaiser Wilhelm* and the *Chateau Yquem*—were still there in 1900.[29] The Italians who had remained in Sunny Side comprised thirty-one families with both father and mother, plus four single-parent families. Sixty-four children were under twelve, thirty-two were over twelve. Twelve children, all still alive, were born at Sunny Side between 1896 and 1900. There seems to be some confusion over place and date of birth of three others.[30] There were ten single persons. These data should be taken with some reservations. The census takers probably did not speak Italian, and many answers may have been incorrect. The names, for example, were misspelled through phonetic transcriptions. A simple name like Mariuccia Reginelli became Marutcha Rudynella, Zibellini became Sibilinia, and Zampa, Zamper.

A comparison of arrival dates and names listed in the 1900 census, and the passenger lists of the *Chateau Yquem* and *Kaiser Wilhelm* reveals that all the families residing in Sunny Side in 1900 were most likely part of the two original groups: ninety-three (51.1%) match names on the *Chateau Yquem* list; thirty-nine (22.3%) match names on the *Kaiser Wilhelm* list; thirty-five (20.0%) approximate names on the *Chateau Yquem* list; and eight (4.6%) approximate names on the *Kaiser Wilhelm* list.

Despite the plantation's problems, emigration from the Marches to Sunny Side resumed after 1900 and continued until World War

---

[28] U.S. Department of Commerce, Records of the Bureau of the Census, RG 29, "Twelfth Census of the United States, 1900," T623 R52.

[29] The families of Albeno Chicalory (Albino Cicchellero), Pianalto Celeste (Celeste Pianalto), and Muscannia Pietro (Pietro Mascagni) were still in Sunny Side when the census was taken, thus invalidating Lemke's affirmation that they were part of the original group of colonists that followed Father Bandini to Tontitown in the spring of 1898. See Lemke, *Tontitown*, p. 17. Giovanna Rosa (Giovanni Roso) and the family of Louis Fellazzarra (Louis Pelizzaro) also left Sunny Side after the census and eventually settled in Rosati, Missouri, where they were included in the list compiled by Schiavo. See Schiavo, *Italians in Missouri*, pp. 152–54.

[30] Cesare Papili's birth was listed as May 1897, Joseph Mascagni's as January 1896, and Elda Cicchellero's as March 1896. In reality the first two arrived on the *Kaiser Wilhelm* and the third aboard the *Chateau Yquem*.

I. These departures were fostered by false promises, since incentives often were given for bringing relatives from Italy to the plantation. The later arrivals traveled in very small groups and are difficult to trace. Reports in the *Bollettino dell'emigrazione* during that time described the conditions of Italians at Sunny Side as a form of slavery. The American government also investigated charges of peonage at Sunny Side. Among those implicated was O.B. Crittenden, but he was acquitted of peonage charges in 1907. Umberto Pierini, a former Sunny Side colonist who became an immigration agent for several Delta cotton growers, was found guilty of bringing Italian families to the cotton plantations in violation of existing labor laws.[31]

Sunny Side was investigated by the U.S. Immigration Commission in 1909. At that time there were still 127 families living on the plantation, a total of about 600 people. The plantation, which comprised 10,000 acres, had only 4,700 acres under cultivation and only 2,700 of those in cotton.[32] The boll weevil struck the area in 1907 and 1910. In 1910 a new management company changed the plantation's agrarian pact; henceforth tenants would pay no rent, and the landlord would receive a quarter of the crop. The Italian tenant farmers despised this idea and slowly began deserting Sunny Side. They went elsewhere in the area and bought land of their own. By the early 1920s no Italians were left in Sunny Side, although most of them remained in the Lake Village vicinity, where they still constitute a visible presence with large properties and activities related to agriculture.[33]

Today in Lake Village only a few families can trace their heritage directly to Sunny Side's first settlers. Nine of the thirty Italian

---

[31] Gerolamo Moroni, "Il peonage nel sud degli Stati Uniti," *Bollettino dell'emigrazione* no. 5 (Rome, 1910); Cav. Scelsi, "Relazione del r. console in Nuova Orleans, cav. Scelsi, circa le condizioni degli emigrati italiani in alcune località di quel distretto consolare, allegati al rendiconto sommario dell'adunanza del 13 dicembre 1907," *Bollettino dell'emigrazione* no. 8 (Rome, 1908), pp. 38–44; Luigi Villari, "Gli Italiani nel sud degli Stati Uniti," *Bollettino dell'emigrazione* no. 10 (Rome, 1907), pp. 39–49; Luigi Villari, "Relazione sugli Italiani nel distretto consolare di Nuova Orleans," *Bollettino dell'emigrazione* no. 20 (Rome, 1907), pp. 1–46; Giacomo Moroni, "L'emigrazione italiana nel distretto consolare di Nuova Orleans," *Bollettino dell'emigrazione* no. 16 (Rome, 1908), pp. 17–25. See also Pete Daniel, *The Shadow of Slavery: Peonage in the South, 1901–69* (Champaign, Ill., 1972).

[32] U.S. Immigration Commission, *Recent Immigrants in Agriculture*, pp. 319–37.

[33] Louis Guida, "Immigrant Farmers: Italians in the Arkansas Delta" (undated ms., copy in E.R. Milani personal papers).

families in Lake Village have family names linked to the plantation. Five of these family names appear both on the passenger manifest of the *Chateau Yquem* and in the 1900 census figures: Reginelli, Alpe, Cingolani, Pierini and Catalani. Four more names do not appear in the census, but were included on one of the passenger lists: Grassi, Marchetti, and Rossini on the *Chateau Yquem* list; and Mazzanti on the *Kaiser Wilhelm* list.

These names prove that what happened ninety years ago is not just legend, though it might seem so to a traveler visiting the site of the old plantation. I toured the site in April 1980, accompanied by Geno Mazzanti, a local farmer who remembers Sunny Side.[34] Geno pointed out a large empty area. He pointed out the locations of the levee, the church, the company office, and the gin. Geno spotted a pecan tree, the only living symbol of those pioneer days, situated just beyond the church site. The grass of the cemetery is mowed by old-timers out of respect; a large metal structure in the form of a cross stands in the middle. Sunny Side is now just a geographical point where so many *Marchigiani* and *Veneti* ended their passage to the New World:

$$33°\quad 21'\quad 20''\quad N,\quad 91°\quad 12'\quad 30''\quad W$$

---

[34] Egino (Geno) Mazzanti was born in Ostra, Ancona, on 2 March 1894. His family was advised to leave for the cotton fields in 1905 by an agent who lived in their village. In 1906 Geno and his family reached a friend who had some land about two miles south of Sunny Side Plantation. In 1908 they moved to a plantation near Red Leaf and in 1920 made a final move to Lake Village. Geno was well known in the area as a successful farmer and landowner. He wrote and read Italian, though he had only three years of school in Italy. He was considered a patriarch among the Italians and the person most aware of what happened in Sunny Side. Egino Mazzanti died 13 March 1984. See also *Farm Credit Report* (St. Louis, July 1938); Egino Mazzanti to E.R. Milani, 1979–1981, Milani personal papers; and State of Arkansas, *Plat Book of Chicot County*, 1973.

Italians in Small Town and Rural Texas

Valentine J. Belfiglio

After 1870 Italian immigration to Texas substantially increased. Between 1870 and 1920, the foreign-born population of Texas grew from 186 to more than 8,000. Immigrants from the *Mezzogiorno*, especially Sicily, settled primarily in the lower Brazos River valley and on the Galveston County mainland between 1870 and 1914, although there were smaller settlements elsewhere.[1] Meanwhile, a few families from *Alta Italia* established farms in Montague County, and hundreds of Italians labored in the coal mines of Thurber and laid railroad tracks between Victoria and Rosenberg.[2] But before coming to Texas to plant corn and cotton, farmers from Sicily spent grueling months cutting sugarcane in Louisiana.

After the American Civil War, Louisiana and other southern states were confronted with a serious labor shortage due to the abolition of slavery and the migration of blacks to the North. To solve the problem, the agricultural leaders of Louisiana decided to invite immigrant

---

[1] See Tables 1 and 2. The information presented in this paper is based on interviews with prominent Italian families, their personal family records, parish records, local newspapers, public documents (tax records, land transactions, censuses), and the resources of the Institute of Texan Cultures at San Antonio and the Texas State Archives at Austin.

[2] J.R. Commons, *Races and Immigrants in America* (New York, 1907), p. 72.

laborers to work on their sugar plantations. In 1866 Louisiana officials created the Bureau of Immigration, which distributed pamphlets describing the resources of the state. But this initial attempt met with only limited success.

In July 1880 the bureau sent an experienced agent to Europe, and he succeeded in contracting several hundred agricultural workers. The Louisiana Sugar Planters' Association agreed to pay the necessary travel and living expenses of the new immigrants.[3] The association preferred Italians because "they were said to be hard-working, thrifty, and content with few comforts."[4] To encourage the immigration of Italians to Louisiana, the Bureau of Immigration, in cooperation with the steamship lines that served New Orleans, established direct passage from Trieste, Palermo, and Naples.[5]

With this accomplished, the number of Italians emigrating to Louisiana began to grow. Of the 3,878 immigrants who arrived there in 1890, 2,611 came from Italy.[6]

The S.S. *Po*, which sailed from Palermo, Sicily, and arrived in New Orleans on 8 December 1891, was one of many immigrant ships carrying a capacity load of 800 to 900 passengers who would make the United States their home. They had few financial resources—seventeen dollars was the average—and many had nothing. The immigrants were crowded into steerage for the crossing, which took several months. Frequently families would separate, sending one or two persons ahead to find work and settle; then other members of the family would join them. Meanwhile, Texas agricultural leaders were also faced with labor shortages in their corn and cotton fields. They offered generous sharecropping terms to entice European immigrants to their state, and many Italians responded.

---

[3] (New Iberia) *Louisiana Sugar Bowl*, 24 February 1881. This weekly newspaper was devoted to the interests of sugar planters, the promotion of immigration, and the development of agriculture in Louisiana.

[4] J. Carlyle Sitterson, *Sugar Country: The Cane Sugar Industry in the South, 1753–1950* (Lexington, Ky., 1953), p. 315.

[5] Louisiana Board of Agriculture and Immigration, *Fifteenth Biennial Report of the Commission of Agriculture and Immigration for the Years 1910–1911* (Baton Rouge, 1912), p. 14.

[6] George E. Cunningham, "The Italians: A Hindrance to White Solidarity in Louisiana, 1890–1898," *Journal of Negro History* 50 (January 1965): 22.

Brazos Valley Italians

Italians came to Texas between 1880 and 1914, primarily to improve their standard of living. Many of them wanted to buy their own farms. The size of the state, the quality of the land, the climate, and the fact that Texas was somewhat closer than California to the large Eastern markets were positive factors. Italians began arriving in the lower Brazos River valley in the early 1870s, when a few families settled near Bryan. While searching the public records of the Office of the District Clerk of Brazos County for the oldest document involving an Italian, the author discovered a license for the marriage of Antonio Saladino and Bechin Mirri dated 2 January 1874.[7]

Businessmen in the Bryan area had long advertised in European newspapers for immigrants to help revitalize the local economy. Immigration was facilitated by the advance of the railroad through Brazos County in 1867–69. In addition, the citizens of the county built an immigration house in Bryan for the convenience of newly arrived settlers. They were allowed to live there free until they could find employment and living quarters.[8] The earliest Italians founded the Agricultural Benevolence Society, with J.M. Saladino as its first president. The society helped other new immigrants make the necessary adjustments to their new environment.[9]

Italians did not begin arriving in Brazos County in large numbers until about 1880. They came primarily from three small farming communities about forty miles south of Palermo—Poggioreale, Corleone and Salapurta.[10] They had first settled in Louisiana, where they cut sugarcane and accumulated some savings. Families made the important decision to move from Louisiana to the Brazos valley because of the opportunity to buy their own land. They sailed to Houston from New Orleans and traveled to Bryan by train. Twenty-four hundred Sicilians, who had worked as section hands on the Houston and Texas railroad, moved to Bryan after their labor was no longer needed

---

[7] Marriage license, 2 January 1874, Office of the District Clerk, Bryan, Tex.

[8] Elmer Grady Marshall, "The History of Brazos County, Texas" (M.A. thesis, University of Texas, Austin, 1937), pp. 108–10.

[9] Lois Alyne Wilcox, "The Early History of Bryan, Texas" (M.A. thesis, University of Texas, Austin, 1952), pp. 81–82.

[10] James and Mary Scarmardo, and Marion J. Scarmardo, interview with author, Bryan, Tex., 22 June 1980. Mary E. Dorsey, *Those Were The Days: Bryan, Brazos County, 1821–1921* (Bryan, Tex., 1976), p. 55.

on that project.[11] At first the new settlers worked as sharecroppers and grew corn, cotton, and other crops to make enough money to buy farms and businesses. According to Johnny Lampo, a lifelong resident of Bryan whose grandfather was one of the original Italian settlers, "The Italians proved that they could, on their own, establish their independence through farming, industry and private enterprise. They never looked for government handouts . . . . The local bank soon found out that the average Italian's word was as good as a signed contract."[12]

Johnny's father, Sam Lampo, said that the success of the Italian people in Texas was due in part to their ability to adapt and their willingness to help one another. "The Italian community was all one family. If a man who had started a crop became ill, we would all pitch in to harvest and sell his corn and cotton. We rendered this service free of charge. When a man lost his mule, the next morning he had another one on his lot. If a family became sick they were fed and cared for by other members of the community."[13]

Italians got along better with the Mexicans of the area than the English-speaking people had. They were both Latin peoples who practiced Catholicism, and it was relatively easy for Italians to learn Spanish. There were also cultural similarities. To all Mediterranean people, food is a symbol of human society and its most basic relationship, the family.[14] Both groups revered the family and practiced patriarchy. The Mexican concept of "virilidad" (manliness), was well understood by Italian males, who knew the term as "virilità."

However, social relations between Mexicans and Italians were kept at a distance. Each group felt that its particular culture was somehow superior to the other, and intermarriage was virtually nonexistent. For the Italians, marriage traditionally took place only among clan members. But there was not complete harmony among the Italians. Sicilians from the town of Corleone settled on the east side of the Brazos River, and those from Poggioreale made their homes on the west side of the river. The groups had been suspicious of each other in Sicily, and this mistrust continued for some time in America. They

---

[11] Andrew F. Rolle, *The Immigrant Upraised* (Norman, Okla., 1968), p. 226.

[12] Johnny and Bonnie Lampo, interview with author, Bryan, Tex., 22 June 1980.

[13] Sam Lampo, interview with author, Bryan, Tex., 22 June 1980.

[14] Herbert J. Gans, *The Urban Villagers* (New York, 1962), p. 33.

spoke different dialects, and worshipped different patron saints. The *Poggiorealesi* prayed to St. Anthony, and the *Corleonesi* prayed to St. Luke. For fifty years, intermarriage was very rare.

The Italians bought flood-prone land in the Brazos River bottoms between Hearne and Bryan. Earlier settlers, including Germans and Czechs, had avoided the land for that reason. The Italians were willing to gamble with disaster in exchange for fertile soil that normally produced abundant crops. They lost badly in 1899 and again in 1900, when devastating floods struck the region. From 27 June to 1 July 1899, a great rainstorm centered over the Brazos River watershed caused the worst flood on record for that area. Between thirty and thirty-five lives were lost, and property damage was estimated at $9 million. Robert Falzone, a lifetime resident of the Brazos valley area and grandson of Giorgio Falzone, one of the original Italian settlers, described the impact of the 1899 flood on his family. "All of the crops were destroyed. Potatoes and onions were especially vulnerable. My family saved themselves by climbing to the roof of their home until help came."[15]

By the 1890s Brazos County had one of the highest concentrations of Italian farmers in the United States. The U.S. census shows that 553 foreign-born Italians lived there in 1900. That year, the *Società di Colonizzazione Italiana del Texas* was in operation. The society bought more than 25,000 acres of land, which it divided into 50-acre lots. The society spent almost a million dollars in a farm development program that featured the purchase of land and acquisition of farm machinery and building materials.

The vast majority of the Italians who came to the United States settled in large cities, where the traditions of the family were greatly altered. In Bryan the situation was different. The patriarchal family unit remained as an accepted way of life to most of the immigrants of the Brazos valley. Few conflicts with tradition existed in Texas compared to the eastern cities where the family unit easily deteriorated. Immigrant women were especially slow to change. Because the Italians lived in colonies, women had little reason to associate with people outside their own group. Unlike the large cities in other parts of the country, the Brazos valley had no factories where Italian women could work and achieve a certain degree of independence from

---

[15] Robert Falzone, interview with author, Marlin, Tex., 21 June 1980.

their husbands. Even domestic service was not available in the area, for only a small number of people could afford maids or household servants.

In 1905 the Italian ambassador visited Texas and was told that the town of Bryan had 3,000 of his countrymen and wished it had ten times that number.[16] The entire population at that time was only 5,000.[17] *The Italian in America*, a book written that year by Eliot Lord, reported that in the

> notable Italian colony at Bryan, Texas, ... a settlement of Sicilians, numbering about twenty-four hundred, has been prospering for several years. The families are spread over the neighborhood to a distance of eighteen miles from the town, and are, for the most part, proprietors of lands chiefly sown with Indian corn and cotton. The families that rent lands generally pay $5.00 a year per acre, and ... the families of the owners and tenants save from $100 to $1,000 yearly, according as they are more or less numerous and economical, and as the crops are more or less abundant. The greater part of these families came originally from Trapani in the neighborhood of Palermo [*sic*], and in point of industry, thrift, good conduct and prosperity, they need not shun comparison with the immigrants from any other part of Italy or from any other country ....
>
> All the chief food supplies are here abundant and cheap, meat selling at five cents a pound. Taxation was said to be exceedingly light. The climate was judged to be fully as good as that of Sicily. There is much fertile land to be obtained for cultivation, and the owners give the use of the land without charge for two years to the farmer who clears it. The settlers cut down the trees, selling the wood at $2.00 per cord, and harvest Indian corn in the first year and cotton in the second.[18]

Antonio Varisco is representative of those robust Italian settlers. He was the son of Biagio Varisco and Maria Zumma of Poggioreale. Antonio was born in New Orleans on 10 June 1878. When he was a year old, the family moved back to Italy, but Antonio returned to the United States in 1906. He had married Dorotea Tritico four years earlier, and the couple gave birth to a son, Brazos, on 12 October 1902. Soon after his arrival in America, Antonio found employment in a *macaroni* factory in Houston. After two months he moved to Bryan and worked for eight months at seventy-five cents a day. Later

---

[16] Institute of Texan Cultures, University of Texas at San Antonio, *The Italian Texans* (San Antonio, 1973), p. 13; Rolle, *The Immigrant Upraised*, p. 227.

[17] Rolle, *The Immigrant Upraised*, p. 227.

[18] Eliot Lord, *The Italian in America* (New York, 1905), pp. 89–90.

he rented 25 acres of land and gradually became the owner of more than 1,000 acres of cotton land.

Brazos Varisco joined his parents in Bryan in 1907. He married Lucille Scardino in 1924 and became an American citizen five years later. Brazos eventually acquired 3,100 acres of land, of which 2,300 acres were devoted to raising cotton. With his father and brother, Giuseppe, he owned a cotton gin with the capacity for producing 2,000 bales of cotton a year. He also owned five airplanes for agricultural spraying. Brazos served as Director of the Bryan Chamber of Commerce and as a member of the Young Men's Club. He was active in civic affairs and charitable movements.[19] Varisco, Texas, a rural community in west Brazos County, and Varisco Airport, which is located in that community, are named in his honor.

Sam Emola was a farmer in Corleone, Sicily, before he brought his family to the United States in 1891. High taxes and the cost of living had made it necessary for him, like most other European immigrants, to look for better conditions. Following many other Sicilians, the Emolas sailed from Palermo to New Orleans, then moved to the Brazos valley. In Brazos County Emola farmed "on the halves" until he saved enough money to purchase his own land.[20]

In 1896 a parish was established for the large number of Italian families who had moved to Bryan. St. Anthony Catholic Church was erected on Polk Avenue. The white frame building served until 1926, when it was destroyed by fire. Most of the Italians who settled in the Brazos valley brought with them a religious custom, the feast of St. Joseph, celebrated on 19 March. St. Joseph is the patron saint of Italy, and particularly of Sicily. The dinner was held during Lent, when no meat was allowed. Therefore, dishes were prepared of fish, pasta, eggs, and vegetables. Fancy cakes and biscuits were elaborately decorated by the women of the church, who worked for days preparing the celebration. On the day before the feast the priest was called to bless the food and drink. On the feast day tradition called for families to invite the poor to their homes to eat. The master of the house would symbolically bathe the feet of the guests, as was done before the Last Supper. After the feast the remaining food was distributed to

---

[19] Giovanni Schiavo, *Italian-American Who's Who*, vol. 7 (New York, 1943), pp. TEX 4, 5.

[20] Dorsey, *Those Were The Days*, p. 43.

the poor. When the Sicilians reached Texas, the custom was altered somewhat because Italians felt awkward about inviting people who could not understand the language or custom. They chose, instead, children of their own families to represent the poor.[21]

No study of the emigrants from the *Mezzogiorno* who settled in Texas would be complete without examining the importance of the role of women. The Italian woman has been the center of the life of the entire ethnic group. The privileges transmitted to her gave her a status that evoked the special position of women in the legend of chivalry. At the same time, the responsibilities, demands, and expectations placed upon her were enormous. The stress that resulted was staggering. As Richard Gambino has aptly put it, "While all Italian Americans feel the poignancy of their inherited sensitivity to the essential hardness of life, the woman experiences it deeply, almost physically, in ways which the male is spared."[22]

The experience of Angela Salvaggio Cangelosi provides an excellent example. Angela Salvaggio was born 5 September 1855, in Poggioreale, province of Trapani. She married Giovanni Cangelosi, and the couple had three sons and two daughters. In the 1880s the family moved to the Brazos County area, where Giovanni's brother, Giuseppe, already lived. The Cangelosis settled in the area known as Mudville, between Mumford, Steele Store, and Stone City, near Bryan. Giovanni purchased about 260 acres of Brazos River bottomland. Angela's life became that of a typical pioneer woman of the day—preparing meals, sewing, washing, cleaning, educating her children, and rearing them in the knowledge of the Savior.

Frank E. Tritico, great-grandson of Angela Salvaggio Cangelosi, describes her life in *Women in Early Texas*:

> Up at dawn, Angela prepared the day's meals and sent breakfast and lunch to the men and boys in the fields by their younger sisters and brothers. The staple Italian meal of *pasta* (spaghetti) had to be rolled by hand and placed in the sun to dry .... Bread was made by hand and baked in outdoor ovens of brick heated by coals. The first year the cooking was done in the fireplace which served as the house's heating unit also. Special grills and cooking pots which sat in coals and had coals heaped above served as cooking utensils. ... Large iron wash pots were placed over fires outdoors. The family's clothes, washed by hand, went into the pot where they were stirred with a stick, rinsed, and

---

[21] Ibid., pp. 24–25.

[22] Richard Gambino, *Blood of My Blood* (New York, 1975), p. 160.

hung in the sun to dry. The soap used had been made by Angela from lye and grease renderings. Later the clothes were ironed by Angela and the girls with flat irons heated in the fireplace or stove.[23]

Tritico points out the many important functions performed by Angela and other dedicated Italian women. Most of the clothes were made at home—dresses, boys' and men's shirts, and even everyday trousers. Lace trim for dresses was crocheted and tatted by the women in the evenings by firelight or lamplight.

> Angela and John were very religious and since there was no church near, they gathered the family and the relatives on Sunday mornings and read the Mass and Gospel from a missal brought from Sicily. Evening devotions were led by Angela after supper in front of the fireplace .... The hardships of pioneering were alleviated in part by the regular Sunday evening dances Angela arranged in her home where one of her sons played the accordion and friends and neighbors brought their adolescents to dance and visit. There were no doctors in the area and Angela was much sought after as a midwife and *doctoressa* [sic]. She made home-remedies and used folk-medicine and herbs in treating her family and those who came to her for help.[24]

Angela died in Houston in 1924.

Around the turn of the century a number of southern Italian farmers settled in the vicinity of Highbank in Falls County. In 1910, Burleson and Robertson Counties also had significant numbers of Italian residents. For the most part, the land of these people is still in family hands. When cotton and other crops became unprofitable for small family farmers, the children moved into the towns of Bryan, Hearne, and Marlin and engaged in other types of businesses. Meanwhile, Italians were also settling on the Galveston County mainland.

Italians of the Galveston County Mainland

Italians from southern Italy began settling on the Galveston County mainland in the late 1890s. While searching parish records in Dickinson, Texas, the author discovered a baptismal certificate for Joseph Pizzitolla, who was baptized on 4 April 1897. He was the son of Gustavo Pizzitolla and Anna Ciulla of Texas City.[25] Many Italians were

---

[23] Evelyn M. Carrington et al., *Women in Early Texas* (Austin, 1975), p. 45.

[24] Ibid., pp. 46–47.

[25] Certificate of baptism, 4 April 1897, Shrine of the True Cross Catholic Church, Dickinson, Tex.

brought to the Galveston County mainland by the Stewart Title Company. Others went there from Bryan to seek relief from the 27 June–1 July 1899 rainstorm. The Italian consular agent, Clemente Nicolini, aided the flood victims in finding new land in Dickinson and elsewhere in Galveston County. For a time, he operated what amounted to a one-man immigration bureau and land development company. Nicolini Street in Dickinson is named in his honor.[26]

In 1905, the Italian government sent its ambassador in Washington, Baron Mayor des Planches, to visit Dickinson and Galveston as part of his trip through the southern United States. His major purpose was to identify suitable resettlement areas for Italians in the northern states who wanted to take advantage of the agricultural opportunities of the South and Southwest.[27] About 200 Brazos valley Italians moved to the Dickinson area. They bought inexpensive land and began growing fruit commercially. During the first and second decades of this century, Italians in Dickinson shipped tens of thousands of cases of strawberries in refrigerated boxcars to markets throughout the Midwest. They also began growing figs in the 1920s.

The families of Francesco Termini, Andrea Magliolo, and Leo Luca Liggio are examples of the many Italians who prospered and made important contributions to Galveston County. Francesco Termini was born in Italy on 28 October 1873; he was thirteen years old when he arrived in America. Later he operated a small grocery store, and when his business expanded he bought and developed a large amount of land in Dickinson and Galveston. Eventually he played an important role in helping develop the business community of Dickinson. Termini Street in Dickinson is named in his honor. Andrea Magliolo came to Galveston in 1905 from Favignana, an island off the west coast of Sicily. When he arrived he was seventeen and spoke no English. Andrea worked as a barber in the shop of his future brother-in-law, Rosario Vassallo, and in 1911 he borrowed enough money to open his own business. In 1909 he married Grazia Vassallo; the couple had five sons and two daughters. Four of the sons became physicians and opened clinics in Dickinson and League City.[28]

Leo Luca Liggio was born in Corleone, Sicily. He married a woman

---

[26] Institute of Texan Cultures, *The Italian Texans*, pp. 22–23.

[27] Jim Hudson, *Dickinson: Taller Than the Pines* (Burnett, Tex., 1979), pp. 87–88.

[28] Ibid., pp. 103–104.

with the first name of Benedetta in 1875, and the couple had three daughters and two sons. Leo and his eldest son, Vincenzo (born in 1876), sailed to New York in 1891. They traveled by train to a small town in Louisiana and worked in a sawmill there for two years. The other members of their family joined them in Louisiana. The Liggios moved to Bryan and worked as sharecroppers until 1899 when they and other Italian families migrated to Dickinson. The men worked for the Galveston, Houston & Henderson Railroad on the track that eventually connected Galveston and Houston. In 1906, Leo and his friend Giuseppe Scalisi purchased ten acres of land on which they grew strawberries and other crops. Leo became a naturalized citizen of the United States in 1913 and opened the first movie theater in Dickinson two years later. His son, Vincenzo, married Paulene Reele on 25 June 1905. Vincenzo became a respected businessman in Dickinson; Liggio Street is named after him.[29]

In 1909 Professor Alberto Pecorini of the American International College, Springfield, Massachusetts, reported that "nearly one thousand Italians reside in the vicinity of Dickinson. They are raising vegetables and berries, and the majority are quite well off; the colony increases very rapidly."[30] Three years later Ambassador Mayor des Planches made another visit to Texas. He indicated that the Italian colony at Dickinson "includes about 100 families, all from the province of Palermo. Each one possesses from four to ten acres of excellent land, well cultivated, worth $100 to $200 per acre."[31] The ambassador found similar settlements at Hitchcock and Galveston. "Galveston has at present about 30,000 inhabitants, of which perhaps 1,200 are Italians."[32]

The Italians of Montague County

Italians from the Alpine provinces of northern Italy began arriving in Montague County in the late 1870s. While searching the county

[29] Josephina Marie Liggio, interview with author, Dickinson, Tex., 6 July 1980; Josephina Marie Liggio, letter to author, 3 August 1980.

[30] Alberto Pecorini, "The Italian As an Agricultural Laborer," *The Annals of the American Academy of Political and Social Science* 33 (January–June 1909): 388.

[31] Edmondo Mayor des Planches, *Attraverso gli Stati Uniti: Per l'emigrazione italiana* (Turin, 1913), pp. 164–68.

[32] Ibid., p. 165.

records and the records of St. Mary's Catholic Church in Henrietta, Texas, the author discovered a certificate of baptism for Rose Fenoglio, the daughter of Jacob (Giacomo) and Domenica Fenoglio, who was born on 26 July 1879 and baptized on 28 September 1893.[33] This is the oldest church record involving Italians in Montague County. The Fenoglios came from the village of Spraco Sano, which is located in the province of Turin. Their ancestors had worked in the coal mines of Valle d'Aosta. Giovanni, Antonio, and Giacomo Fenoglio left Italy to make more money and improve their standard of living. They sailed to New York from Le Havre, France, and first went to Braidwood, Illinois, to find work in the coal mines. From there they moved to Lehigh, Oklahoma, and again worked in the coal mines.

The coal deposits that attracted Italian immigrants were not developed in Oklahoma until the 1870s. The first Italians entered the region in 1875; between 200 and 300 lived in the area in 1883. Pittsburg County had the highest number of foreign-born residents in the coal producing area and the second highest in the state, with 3,367 listed in 1910. Of these foreign-born residents the Italians were by far the largest single nationality, numbering 1,398. The principal Italian colony in the county, as well as in the state, was in Krebs. Coal County ranked second in the number of Italian settlers. Lehigh, where the Fenoglio family worked, was established in 1880 as the first coal camp in that county. Mine owners moved the site several times, eventually locating the permanent town in 1884. Two years later Coalgate was founded. Although immigrants were not as dominant in Coalgate as they were in Krebs, the foreign stock numbered 1,206 out of 3,255. Other nearby towns, such as Phillips and Midway, soon developed. As in Pittsburg County, Italians were the largest group, numbering 443; including the second generation and several Italians from the Austrian Tyrol, approximately 700 lived in the county.

Living conditions in the coal mining communities of Oklahoma were not good, particularly during the days when Oklahoma was an Indian territory. Italians and other coal miners were exposed to smallpox, cholera, and other epidemic diseases. There was a shortage of water, and the summers were hot and dry. There were also periodic skirmishes with renegade Indians. When the first Italians came to the area, few houses were available. As a result, the miners were almost to-

---

[33] Certificate of baptism, 28 September 1893, St. Mary's Catholic Church, Henrietta, Tex.

tally dependent on the mining company to meet their material needs. They lived in company houses and were sometimes paid in scrip good only in the company store. The houses were usually one-story, one-family dwellings with three to five rooms. Poorly built with cheap lumber, these houses were little more than shacks.[34]

Giovanni, Antonio, and Giacomo Fenoglio became dissatisfied with the living and working conditions in Lehigh. Like the Sicilian settlers of the Brazos valley, these Alpine Italians developed a strong desire to farm their own land. In 1876 three families, headed by the two Fenoglio brothers and Barretto Raimondi, moved from Oklahoma to Pilot Grove, a small community in Grayson County, Texas.[35] This small group settled on 640 acres of land, which they thought they had purchased. But after paying most of the $3,000 agreed upon for a section of the land, it became apparent that the three men had been swindled and did not have title to the property they had cleared and worked. Unable to speak English well, without legal counsel, they gave up their claim and headed west to Wichita Falls.

The three families stopped to rest near Montague, and were attracted to the area; its sandy soil was perfect for vineyards, orchards, and vegetable farms. Thus, Montague County became their home. Despite the problem of maintaining an adequate supply of water to meet the needs of both their families and their crops, the group prospered. They wrote to their kinfolk and friends about the excellent agricultural opportunities of the area. These people were impressed, and some of them migrated to Montague, Bowie, and Nocona. Pete Belisario moved from Osage City, Kansas, to Montague in 1890; Tony Rossi also went there that year. Giovanni Carminati, Paul Veretto, and Pete Carminati and their families arrived shortly thereafter. Around 1900, other Italians settled in the area. Among them were the families of John Vitali, Decio Gasparini, Andrew Pelligrenelli, Edward Aragoni, Bartolo Salvi, and Battista Salvi.[36]

Giovanni Carminati was typical of these settlers. He was born in Bergamo, near Milan, on 29 January 1875. While in Italy he had worked as a day laborer for fifteen to thirty cents a day. Giovanni

---

[34] Kenny L. Brown, *The Italians in Oklahoma* (Norman, Okla., 1980), pp. 12, 14, 42.

[35] Melvin Fenoglio, interview with author, Montague, Tex., 29 June 1980.

[36] Melvin Fenoglio, "Strangers in a Strange Land," in Alva B. Copeland et al., *Panorama of Nocona's Trade Area* (Saint Jo, Tex., 1976), p. 122.

arrived in Kansas by way of New York about 1887 and labored in the coal mines of Pittsburg. He moved to Montague in the early 1890s, where he met and married Marietta Tonetti. The couple had eight children. In Montague the family cut down trees, sold the wood, and then bought a small farm. For a time, Giovanni served as a trustee of the local school.[37]

The lives of these new citizens revolved around agriculture. They produced luscious concord grapes, apples, peaches and a variety of vegetables. The Italian settlers originally purchased the land for six to eight dollars an acre with mineral rights included. Oil discoveries on several tracts have since enhanced property values considerably.[38] Some of the original settlers became grocers, butchers, and carpenters. Most of these immigrants were devout Catholics, and in 1901 they established St. John's Catholic Church in Montague. Before a church was built, regular services were held in various homes. A priest occasionally visited the community and offered mass. This was an opportunity for baptisms, marriages, and other church rituals. Sometimes, a temporary altar was set up outdoors to accommodate large gatherings for Sunday worship.

The Italian colony in Montague reached a peak in 1910 with 69 foreign-born residents. In the first quarter of the twentieth century the total population of Italian immigrants and their families was estimated at 300. Most of these people were hardworking, law-abiding citizens. But they sometimes felt the prejudices of their Protestant neighbors, who were suspicious of their customs and religious practices. According to Melvin Fenoglio, a lifetime resident of Montague, "Despite their encounters with hardships in establishing a new home in an alien environment, the majority of the early new citizens possessed a happy temperament. Courageous in facing their many problems, forthright in their responsibilities as citizens, and optimistic in their outlooks toward the future, they began to bridge the gap which separated them and their American neighbors."[39]

At first, the Italians associated almost exclusively with members of their own group. Marriage took place only among clan members. But that practice was gradually abandoned by later generations. Weekly dances were a favorite form of diversion; couples danced to the

---

[37] Joe Louis Carminati, interview with author, Montague, Tex., 16 July 1980.

[38] Institute of Texan Cultures, *The Italian Texans*, pp. 15–16.

[39] Fenoglio, "Strangers," p. 123.

The **Barney Fenoglio homestead near Montague.** Photo courtesy of Mrs. C.P. Nabours; copy courtesy of University of Texas Institute of Texan Cultures.

codiglione, a folk dance common in some parts of *Alta Italia*. In the beginning, dances were closed to outsiders. But they gradually became integrated into the local community, as Italian dances were replaced by contemporary American dances. Men played *bocce* and *morra* regularly on Sunday afternoons, especially in the summer.[40] It was customary for families to take turns preparing huge feasts, which included many kinds of food and wine. A typical offering might include *minestrone alla milanese* (vegetable soup, Milanese style), *stracotto* (pot roast), *polenta e osei* (a cornmeal dish with a sauce of tiny wild birds), and *risotto* (a rice dish cooked in broth). The food ordinarily was accompanied by homemade wine made from concord grapes. A favorite dessert was *zabaglione* (a sweet made with beaten eggs and Marsala wine). All clan members were invited, and after dinner the games began.

Although the Italians of Montague County initially clung to the security of their native language and customs, they gradually began to adapt to their new environment. Realizing that Texas was now their home, they slowly assimilated the local culture and mores. Italians enrolled their children in public schools, encouraged them to learn the English language, and instilled in them a feeling of patriotism for America. For the most part, the farmland of these settlers has been retained in family hands. But the Italians of Montague County have also become leaders in business, industry, and the professions. Tony Fenoglio served in the Texas legislature from 1951 to 1961; Melvin Fenoglio was superintendent of the Montague Independent School District in the 1970s and early 1980s.

Minor Italian Colonies

At the beginning of World War I, Texas had about 15,000 Italians, two-thirds of whom were engaged in agriculture. In addition to the major colonies around Bryan, Dickinson, and Montague, there were smaller settlements in Texas. Near Houston a hundred families grew vegetables and fruits; many of them owned the lands they cultivated. Italian families were also successful truck farmers near Dallas and Austin. Nicola Negro and the Destefno brothers are examples of early

---

[40] *Bocce* resembles lawn bowling. In *morra*, two people simultaneously extend some of the fingers of one hand, and immediately exclaim a number from zero to ten. The person who guesses the sum of the extended fingers is the winner.

Italian pioneers who settled in the Dallas area. Nicola Negro arrived in Dallas in 1887 and established a large produce business. He was one of the first to recommend the refrigeration of bananas in transit and he received the first refrigerated shipment of the fruit from New Orleans. Francesco and Achille Destefno came to Texas in 1873 and made a small fortune in the wholesale fruit and produce business in Dallas.[41]

In San Antonio about a hundred families worked on small farms near the city. Frank Talerico arrived in San Antonio in 1888 and opened a fruit stand in the business district. In a short time he owned fifteen such stands, all operated by friends and relatives he brought over from Italy. Eventually he built a substantial warehouse from which his chain stores were supplied. Talerico was born at Spezzano della Sila, Calabria, in 1860. Correspondence with a friend in Texas inspired him to seek his fortune there. Talerico became one of the most prominent leaders of the small Italian colony in San Antonio. He died in 1934 at the age of 74.[42]

In southeastern Texas some Italians grew rice, and others became vineyardists in the neighborhood of Gunnison.[43] The only licensed winery in Texas is operated by the Qualia (Quaglia) family on Hudson Road in Del Rio. The enterprise was started in 1883 by Frank and Mary Quaglia, who wanted to make wine for family consumption as they had done in their old home near Milan, Italy. About 5,000 gallons are produced annually from an eighteen-acre tract.[44]

Conclusion

Attracted to Texas because of the opportunity to buy and farm their own lands, Italians have contributed much to the agricultural development of the state. Italian Texans living in small towns and rural areas have for the most part been assimilated into the dominant southern Anglo-American culture. Most of the traditional attitudes of the *contadini* of the *Mezzogiorno* are no longer held today by the Italians living in Bryan and Dickinson. Feelings of *campanilismo* (localism),

---

[41] Institute of Texan Cultures, University of Texas at San Antonio, *Dallas Pioneers*, (San Antonio, 1979), p. 6.

[42] Institute of Texan Cultures, *The Italian Texans*, p. 18.

[43] Rolle, *The Immigrant Upraised*, p. 226; Pecorini, "The Italian As an Agricultural Laborer," p. 388.

[44] Institute of Texan Cultures, *The Italian Texans*, p. 17.

the distrust of outsiders, a negative attitude toward education, and political apathy have largely disappeared. However, modern Italian Texans living in small towns and rural areas are still concerned primarily with local political, economic, and social issues. Although a few of these people have held local political offices and seats in the Texas House of Representatives, none has been nominated for statewide or national office.

In spite of the assimilation process, Italian Texans living in small towns and rural areas retain some distinctive cultural traits. Ethnic identity is often related to membership in the Roman Catholic church, pride in the achievements of Italy in the fields of music and art, some knowledge of the Italian language, knowledge of Italian cuisine, and familiarity with Italian games, dances, and other forms of entertainment. In addition, attachment to family and devotion to the *vicinato* (neighborhood) remain strong among most third-generation Italians living in Bryan, Dickinson, and Montague. But research indicates that an Italian consciousness does not depend exclusively upon any combination of these factors. They merely facilitate the formation and maintenance of an ethnic identity. What is essential to Italian ethnicity is a group perception of having accomplished important things in the past and the desire to accomplish them in the future.

Ethnic identity among Italian Texans depends on common values and sympathies. It exists when people share a common outlook, agree that they are a distinct group, and feel connected to each other. Italian Texans living in small towns and rural areas today still form clubs based on their ethnic identification. These groups host festivals, dinners, *bocce* tournaments, family reunions, and mutual aid programs, and also participate in church activities and civic events. Most Italian Texans are proud of their ancestry. They are also proud of their contributions toward making Texas a better place to live.

Table 1. Foreign-born Italians resident in Texas, 1870–1920.

Year	Number of Italians
1870	186
1880	539
1890	2,107
1900	3,942
1910	7,190
1920	8,024

Source: U.S. census, 1870–1920.

Table 2. Italian population of five selected Texas counties, 1900.

County	Number of Italians
Galveston	560
Brazos	553
Erath	429
Harris	392
Bexar	316
Others	1,692
Total	3,942

Source: U.S. Census Office, *Twelfth Census of the United States, 1900*, vol. 1, *Population* (Washington, D.C., 1901), pp. 783–86.

Itinerant Grimaldesi: Paesani on the Railways of North America

John Potestio

Writing about the Grimaldese emigrants is not an easy task. In the last one hundred years several thousand *Grimaldesi* have migrated to nearly all parts of the Western world. Indeed, it is precisely this dispersion that makes the task of historical reconstruction arduous. Documentary evidence is scarce. The Italian government and Italian historians have shown little interest in the lives of these humble people. However, on this side of the Atlantic some encouraging research is now being done. In Canada, with the impetus of the officially recognized policy of multiculturalism, ethnic history is making significant strides. More and more, historians and sociologists are paying attention to the role played by immigrants in the development of our nation.

This paper is a modest attempt to shed some light on the history of some of the *Grimaldesi* who came to North America at the turn of the twentieth century. As usual, the availability of historical sources dictated the direction of this paper. Frank Iacino, a *Grimaldese* himself, told me that he had some papers I might find useful. It turned out that they were the early records of a railway building company founded by two *Grimaldesi* at the turn of the century.

Because of the few available sources, this paper will likely pose more questions than it answers. The whole issue of whether the Grimaldese sojourning experience in North America is typical of that of other southern Italians who emigrated between 1880 and World War I remains largely unanswered. Nevertheless, the paper may help to determine the historical experience of a group of people who at the time represented a rather large percentage of the *Grimaldesi* who came to North America.

Perched on one of the many hills of the Calabrian Apennines, thirty kilometers south of Cosenza, lies the town of Grimaldi. Aside from its rather aristocratic name, Grimaldi was—and in many ways still is—a nondescript agglomeration of peasant huts.[1] Fearful of the ravages of malaria and the destruction of marauding bands, the *Grimaldesi*, like most other *contadini* of southern Italy, chose the high ground, thereby exposing their homes to the dangers of earthquakes. Indeed, the "old" Grimaldi, razed by a devastating quake, is prominently featured in Grimaldese lore and is a potent force in the imagination of the young.

The people of Grimaldi struggled against nature, eking out a meager living from the unyielding soil. Most were engaged in a losing battle against *latifondisti* and *padroni*, the patronizing bourgeois elite, and the self-serving clergy. The *mezzadri*'s struggle to obtain a more equitable share in return for their backbreaking labor in picking the only abundant crop—chestnuts—usually ended in failure.[2] The *carabinieri* quickly intervened on the side of the landlords. Nor were the nascent workers' associations able to redress their legitimate grievances, since they fell under the leadership of moderate and legalistic bourgeois groups.[3]

The peasantry remained powerless in the face of exploitation because it failed to develop any sense of class solidarity.[4] Periodically the

---

[1] For a detailed account of peasant agglomeration, see Anton Blok, "South Italian Agro-Towns," in *Comparative Studies in Society and History*, vol. 11 (Cambridge, 1969).

[2] Vincenzo Brescia (born in Grimaldi, 1898), interview with author, 8 August 1978.

[3] Enrico Esposito, *Il movimento operaio in Calabria: L'egemonia borghese* (Cosenza, 1977), p. 9.

[4] For an enlightening explanation of peasant psychology in terms of class struggle, see Antonio Gramsci, *La questione meridionale* (Rome, 1973), pp. 64–65.

Grimaldesi would give vent to their anger through desperate, yet pathetic, acts of defiance. Planting lupine seeds in the town square—the favorite place for a promenade for the town's *padroni*—seems in retrospect an angry, spontaneous act rather than a revolutionary one.[5] The more common course of action for the impecunious, oppressed, and exploited *Grimaldesi* was emigration.

Early emigration records for Grimaldi are in a state of disarray. Careful examination of the existing documents, however, reveals some rather useful information, though one has to proceed with caution because of serious gaps. It is not clear when the earliest emigrants departed from Grimaldi; presumably the town followed the same pattern that history, geography, and circumstances imposed on the rest of southern Italy.

Until 1886, the majority of emigrants were from northern Italy, most of them leaving from Veneto. In southern Italy emigration was restricted to a few zones in Basilicata and Calabria. Yet significant numbers of people were also leaving the southern provinces, so that as early as 1867 emigration was considered an "effective substitute for brigandage."[6] By the 1890s emigration had become an exodus. So great were the numbers leaving that the entire psychology about the southern Italian diaspora was changing. Not only was emigration regarded as a necessity to escape the miseries of the south, it had become an obligation.[7]

Documentary evidence of the first Grimaldese emigrants has not been found. It is logical to assume, however, that emigration from Grimaldi followed chronologically that of the coastal regions. We do know that a few *Grimaldesi* were in the United States by the early 1800s.[8] The emigration flow continued uninterrupted until 1915, when the war temporarily halted it. The exodus was directed toward the United States, but some emigrants listed Canada or Brazil as their destination. From 1901 to 1915 an average of more than 80 people a

---

[5] There is some evidence that the *Grimaldesi* participated in the 1848 rebellions led by some *carbonari* from the nearby town of Altilia.

[6] Fernando Manzotti, *La polemica sull'emigrazione nell'Italia unita* (Milan, 1969), p. 13.

[7] Francesco Coletti, "L'emigrazione," in Rosario Villari, ed., *Il Sud nella storia d'Italia*, vol. 1 (Bari, 1972), p. 414.

[8] John Potestio, "From Navvies to Contractors: The History of Vincenzo and Giovanni Veltri, Founders of R.F. Welch Ltd., 1885–1931" (M.A. thesis, Lakehead University, Thunder Bay, Ont., 1981), p. 29.

year applied for their passports, the number fluctuating from a high of 160 in 1903 to a low of 7 in 1915. The population of Grimaldi at that time was about 3,000. The vast majority of emigrants were male. Only 133 of the 1,911 applicants for passports from 1901 to 1915 were female—about 11 percent of the total emigration. During the same period, only twenty-seven families indicated their intention to emigrate to North America. Given the economic and social conditions of southern Italy, it is not surprising to find that 90 percent of the male emigrants were *contadini*. The remaining 10 percent were shoemakers, tailors, and carpenters, with a small number of tinkers, musicians, watchmakers, barbers, and masons.[9]

A closer examination of the emigration data for Grimaldi confirms another aspect of southern Italian emigration: its ravenous appetite for youth. Sixty-one percent of all those who left were thirty years of age or younger. Of these, 35 percent were twenty-one or younger; only 10 percent of the emigrants were over 40. It was not unusual for a thirteen-year-old to apply for a passport, although minors had to be accompanied by an adult during their voyage. Incredible as it may seem today, boys less than ten years old ended up as water boys on the North American railways.[10] Fifteen- and sixteen-year-olds were numerous. A typical Grimaldese emigrant at the turn of the century was male, twenty years old, nearly illiterate and largely unskilled, whose destination was New York.

It should be kept in mind that the designation of New York as the place of destination on a passport did not necessarily imply permanent residence. Although some remained in the great metropolis, most considered it merely the port of entry. From here they dispersed to wherever work was to be found. If not bound for New York, the Grimaldese *contadini* left for (listed in order of frequency): Colorado, Canada, Washington, Utah, and Idaho. A few listed Brazil as their destination.[11]

---

[9] Ibid., p. 12.

[10] In 1901, nine-year-old Francesco Sdao, a *Grimaldese*, came to the United States with his father, ostensibly to find employment. Francesco Sdao, interview with author, 25 July 1979.

Not all young *Grimaldesi*, however, were destined for the work camps. In 1910 Michele Iacino came to Brigham City with his father at the age of fifteen. His father was enlightened enough to send the boy to school rather than to work in the mines. Alessandro Iacino, interview with author, 24 August 1981.

[11] Grimaldi emigration records, 1901–1915.

What happened to these people once they reached the New World? Two factors must be considered. To begin with, Italian immigrants entered a rather hostile milieu. The dominant groups on either side of the 49th parallel displayed a crass xenophobia largely directed toward central and southern Europeans.[12] Americans expressed doubt about the moral fiber of Italians and clamored for "heroic measures" to curb Italian immigration.[13] If we add another problem—the lack of skills of the vast majority of these immigrants—then it becomes clear why the *Grimaldesi* found it difficult to join the mainstream of North American society.[14]

Under the circumstances, it is not surprising that many Italian workers succumbed to the apparent advantages that padronism offered, while frequently becoming victims of the worst features of this peculiar relationship.[15] Because work on the North American railways required strength, endurance, and tolerance of subhuman conditions, *contadini* could easily be transformed into railway workers. To exchange a mattock for a shovel or a *padrone* for a boss did not require a radical change. Hundreds of *Grimaldesi* accepted this change all the more easily because two of their *paesani* had by the late 1890s established a small railway building company.

The history of Vincenzo and Giovanni Veltri, two *Grimaldesi* who came to the United States between 1880 and 1885, cannot be told within the confines of this paper. Briefly, in a span of less than two decades—a period of apprenticeship spent working on the railways of the American Northwest—the elder brother, Vincenzo, founded the

---

[12] Potestio, "From Navvies to Contractors," pp. 30–33.

[13] J.H. Senner (U.S. Commissioner of Immigration), "Immigration from Italy," *North American Review* 142 (May 1896): 649. Other official reports expressed a serious concern about the unassimilable nature of Italians. See U.S. Immigration Commission, *Reports of the Immigration Commission*, vol. 1, *Abstracts*, 61st. Cong., 3d sess., S. Doc. no. 747 (Washington, D.C., 1911), p. 571.

[14] It should be remembered, however, that for various reasons Italian immigration at the turn of the century was not permanent. See Robert F. Foerster, *The Italian Emigration of Our Times* (Cambridge, Mass., 1919), p. 39.

[15] For more detailed information on padronism, see Robert F. Harney, "The Padrone and the Immigrant," *Canadian Review of American Studies* 5 (Fall 1974): 101–118. See also Edwin Fenton, "Immigrants and Unions: A Case Study: Italians and American Labor, 1870–1920" (Ph.D. diss., Harvard University, 1957); and Canada Department of Labour, *The Royal Commission Appointed to Inquire into the Immigration of Italian Labourers to Montreal and the Alleged Fraudulent Practices of Employment Agencies* (Ottawa, 1905).

Raffaele Veltri (right) and a Grimaldese worker on an R.F. Welch Co. railroad gang. Photo courtesy of John Potestio.

J.V. Welch Company.[16] It was not easy for a *contadino* to break through the sociocultural barriers of North American society and become an entrepreneur. Vincenzo had only one advantage—his literacy, a considerable edge at a time when illiteracy among southern Italians was nearly universal. But luck was also on his side. In 1887, Serra and Dini, two Italian contractors from San Francisco, asked Vincenzo to try to restore harmony among workers who had come perilously close to violence after they discovered they had been paid with worthless checks by one of Serra and Dini's subcontractors. Vincenzo proved his mettle. Having obtained a promise from the head contractors that in the future the workers would be paid in gold and paper currency, he persuaded the workers to remain on the job. That success and his considerable experience as a foreman (he had worked for the Montana Central Railway near Butte and had also done some work with other *Grimaldesi* clearing land for the mills and kilns and building rail lines at Anaconda) put Vincenzo in a favorable position for leadership among his *paesani*.

By the end of the 1880s—after he anglicized his name to Welch—Vincenzo decided to venture into the railway building business. When he learned that a railway line was being built in Montana from Butte to Jefferson, he approached Keefer and Company to obtain some work for himself and his brother Giovanni and also to intercede for many of his *paesani*. Vincenzo was successful again; he received the best piece of work on the line. The pattern was established; the *Grimaldesi* had found in one of the *paesani* a man who could provide them with steady employment.

A superficial examination of this relationship might suggest that the *Grimaldesi* had become victims of the *padrone* system. The evidence, however, argues against that view. It is true that through the years the J.V. Welch Company grew and prospered, but this was a normal business development made possible by the astute judgment and hard work of the company's owners. Furthermore, it can be shown that the Grimaldese workers profited from their continuous association with bosses (Giovanni had subsequently become a full partner in the company) whom they knew personally and with whom they could deal on a personal basis.[17] Not only were they assured of a job (the records show that aside from the war years, 1914–1917, *Grimaldesi*

---

[16] Potestio, "From Navvies to Contractors."

[17] Conviviality and the willingness of Italians (as well as other ethnic groups)

were employed continuously on several projects, not all of them rail-way work[18]), they were also provided with the meager provisions so common among the navvies of the early twentieth century.[19] In 1897, Vincenzo had decided to provide a commissary for his workers. The daybooks for the years 1897–1900 show that most of the Veltri brothers' clients were *Grimaldesi*. Even in this respect the Grimaldese workers and bosses found it advantageous to deal with each other: the Veltri brothers reaped some financial gains while their *paesani* were often able to buy food and equipment on credit.

By the late 1890s the *Grimaldesi*, working for their *paesani*, had become a highly mobile, cohesive, homogeneous group ready to fol-low the Welch operation wherever work was to be found. Therefore, when railway contracts could be obtained with greater regularity[20] in British Columbia than in the American Northwest, the entire Welch gang crossed the border. Many *Grimaldesi* worked on several lines in the interior of British Columbia. They remained in the Kootenay area until 1899 when Vincenzo, conscious of shifting fortunes in the railway business, decided to move his operation to northwestern On-tario. Once again the Grimaldese workers entrusted their uncertain futures to the proven *modus operandi* of the Veltris. Their decision was not that of novices who might have been easily persuaded to fol-low an uncharted course; they were veterans of the difficult lives of the navvies. They had endured severe cold, tormenting mosquitoes, and all the discomforts of tent life. They had learned the danger of their work when a *paesano* was killed in an explosion.[21] But they

---

to work with people of their own kind represent an additional response to repre-hensible working conditions. See Edmund Bradwin, *The Bunkhouse Man* (1928; reprint ed., Toronto, 1972), p. 110.

[18] One such unusual project was the construction of a small canal sixty miles from Spokane, Wash. See Welch Papers, in author's possession.

[19] More so than other ethnic groups Italians were known for their frugality. Often they cooked in pairs in an attempt to minimize food costs. See Bradwin, *Bunkhouse Man*, p. 134. Giovanni Veltri's own provisions for the month of Septem-ber 1897 were similar to those of other *Grimaldesi*: three cans of tomatoes, ten pounds of potatoes, fourteen pounds of flour, one can of milk, nine pounds of ham, one pound of lard, and one bar of soap. See Potestio, "From Navvies to Contractors," p. 83.

[20] For a detailed analysis of the struggle among several railway companies for supremacy in the commercial exploitation of the "Inland Empire," see F.W. Howay et al., *British Columbia and the United States* (New York, 1942), pp. 229–54.

[21] Railway building—particularly blasting operations—took a heavy toll. See

had also enjoyed success. A few had become foremen; most had been recognized as reliable, hardworking individuals. After all, had they not built lines over some of the most difficult terrain in North America? It would have been easy for them to remain in British Columbia. But the bond between countrymen proved too strong to be forsaken for mere convenience.[22] Furthermore, the Veltris had not only provided the employment that was so crucial to their well-being, they had also demonstrated their ability to retain the loyalty of their employees and to recruit other *Grimaldesi*. The two brothers knew of the whereabouts of some of their *paesani* and would often inform them of the availability of work on their contracts. Not infrequently the workers would take advantage of such offers and join the Welch crew from distant points in the United States and Canada.[23] As a result, most of the *Grimaldesi* left British Columbia and headed for the wilderness of northern Ontario.

The crowning achievement of the Grimaldese navvies working for Vincenzo and Giovanni Veltri occurred in 1907. Employing 135 men, most of whom were *Grimaldesi*, the Welch Company obtained a substantial contract from the National Transcontinental Railway. The work involved the construction of a line fifty-eight miles long running east of Winnipeg. The Welch Company was responsible for the clearing, grubbing, grading, embankment protection, and all the other work below grade necessary to complete the embankment on the line. The successful completion of this work demonstrated that the *Grimaldesi* had undergone a remarkable metamorphosis: the *contadini* from a small town in Calabria had become railway builders in the New World.

The magnitude of the Transcontinental contract dictated the course that the Welch Company and its Grimaldese workers would take in the next few years. Vincenzo and Giovanni purchased additional equipment and supplies totaling $116,548, a considerable sum for a small contracting firm. The Veltri brothers would have to get substantial returns to offset this outlay. Their crew and equipment could not remain idle for too long, nor would it be profitable to seek work at lo-

---

Donald Avery, *"Dangerous Foreigners"* (Toronto, 1979), p. 36.

[22] There appears to be a natural tendency for immigrant workers who come from the same village to stick together and frequently work on the same project. See Andrew F. Rolle, *The Immigrant Upraised* (Norman, Okla., 1968), p. 155.

[23] Francesco Sdao, interview with author, 25 July 1979.

cations which would necessitate expensive hauls. Hence, from 1907 to 1913 the Grimaldese workers remained in northern Ontario working on several contracts for the Canadian Pacific Railway. Vincenzo's unexpected death and the outbreak of World War I changed the fortunes of the Welch Company and the Grimaldese workers and foremen who had remained with their *paesani* bosses for so long. With Vincenzo's death, the company fell into the less experienced hands of his brother, Giovanni Veltri. After the war began, the number of railway building contracts diminished considerably.

Conclusion

Because of the paucity of historical sources on *Grimaldesi* as well as the lack of historiography on subjects of this nature, conclusions must necessarily be tentative. However, a few observations can be advanced with some certainty. One of the most striking characteristics of the *Grimaldesi* who emigrated at the turn of the century is that, ironically, their latent talents and energies came to fruition not within the tutelage of the newly formed Italian state, but outside it. Even the supportive, civilizing impact of a family was absent from their lives. Not only did the *Grimaldesi* have to fight against the hostile attitude of the receiving society, they also had to overcome the potentially psychologically destructive environment of the frontier.[24] To their credit, most were temperate, frugal, industrious, and faithful to their families. That a few never returned to their wives and children, having succumbed to an "easy" and dissolute life, should surprise no one.

The *Grimaldesi* responded to the North American challenge by taking advantage of the two most readily available opportunities: intermediarism and paesanism. The former was provided by two of their kind who assisted these men by facilitating their search for work. The latter was a natural outgrowth of the immigrant yearning for the familiar. Intermediarism and paesanism made it possible for the *Grimaldesi* to remain and work on the railways of North America for a considerable length of time. Hence, theirs was not an urban experience, but rather an adaptation to frontier conditions. By and large, *Grimaldesi* were not urban settlers but sojourners.

---

[24] S.D. Clark makes it clear that in the absence of traditional institutions and family influence, men fall prey to "personal disorganization." S.D. Clark, *The Developing Canadian Community* (Toronto, 1968), p. 11.

Most *Grimaldesi* returned changed men,[25] some of them extremely rich by village standards.[26] One of them, Gaetano Iachetta (he had formed an early partnership with Vincenzo Veltri), even invested his hard-earned money in a potentially risky venture: bringing electricity to his village. Most others used their money to repair the ancestral home or add to their small and scattered parcels of land. Yet, the greatest service to their town would profit only future generations. The few who remained in the United States or Canada would eventually act as a magnet—a point of reference—which had great significance in establishing a pattern of village chain migration.[27] The *Grimaldesi* have been in touch with returning *Americani* for nearly a century.[28] There is hardly a family that has not been affected by the emigration to North America. Emigration is part of their normal existence.

More importantly, the *Grimaldesi* who provided a reliable pool of labor for the Welch Company ensured the company's growth during a critical period, so that when the second great wave of emigration began after World War II, hundreds of other *Grimaldesi* would emigrate to Canada with an employment visa from the Welch Company to work on the railways, this time for the Canadian National Railways. To impecunious *Grimaldesi*, unable to muster enough cash to buy a ticket to Canada, the Welch contract was the only means of escape from a difficult economic situation.[29] As a result, the *Grimaldesi* of Thunder Bay, Ontario, represent one of the clearest examples of village chain migration. More than 125 families whose roots are in Grimaldi live in Thunder Bay today. Many of the heads of these fam-

---

[25] The theme of the "transformation" of immigrants because of their experience in the New World has been examined by many historians. See Ingrid Semmingsen, "Emigration and the Image of America in Europe," in Henry Steele Commager, ed., *Immigration and American History* (Minneapolis, 1961), p. 53.

[26] Alessandro Iacino (born in Grimaldi, 1913), interview with author, 10 August 1981.

[27] It is no coincidence that today groups of *Grimaldesi* are found precisely where the Welch crew worked in the early part of the twentieth century. Such locations as Spokane, Wash., Butte, Mont., Portland, Ore., Trail, B.C., and Winnipeg, Man., were magnets—points of reference which would have great significance in establishing the pattern of village chain migration in these areas.

[28] Even today this term is used generically to refer to people who have lived either in the United States or Canada.

[29] The contract stipulated that the Welch Company would provide employment for the worker and transportation to the work site, provided that he work for the Canadian National Railways for two years.

ilies worked for the Welch Company at a time when its most lucrative operation was based in Thunder Bay, the company's headquarters.[30]

The legacy of the *Grimaldesi* seems to be universal among peasantry—the indomitable spirit of survival. The penniless *contadini* responded to the hostile and unfamiliar socioeconomic conditions of North American society at the turn of the century by becoming sojourners. The social reality of the time turned *Grimaldesi* into migrant workers who could not sink roots anywhere. Grimaldese workers were found in places where manual labor was required, hence their presence in railway and mining camps. Several decades later, when conditions improved, *Grimaldesi* finally became permanent settlers, primarily in Canada.

---

[30] Port Arthur and Fort William, the two components of the city of Thunder Bay, were joined in 1970. Port Arthur was the Welch Company's headquarters.

Immigrant Friulani in North America

John Zucchi

One group of Italians that has been ignored by ethnic and immigration historians in North America is the *Friulani* (from Friuli in northeastern Italy). Although their numbers in North America were not great before 1930, their dispersion throughout Canada and the United States and their ability to find a niche in the economies of cities, small towns, and rural areas make the *Friulani* an interesting subject for a case study of the migration of skills specific to a region.

A portrayal of *Friulani* in North America must be considered against the background of their earlier temporary migrations throughout Europe. Before the *Friulani* reached the United States, permanent migration meant either settlement in an agricultural colony—usually in Argentina or Brazil—or work in the building trades or as brick makers in Argentina, Brazil, and to a lesser extent Rumania.[1] Emigration to the United States and Canada was an extension of earlier temporary migrations to France, Germany, Austria-Hungary, Ruma-

---

[1] See Lodovico Zanini, *Friuli migrante* (1932; reprint ed., Udine, 1964); Gino and Alberto di Caporiacco, *1887–1880 Coloni friulani in Argentina, in Brasile, Venezuela, Stati Uniti* (Udine, 1978); Gino di Caporiacco, *Storia e statistica dell'emigrazione dal Friuli e dalla Carnia,* 2 vols. (Udine, 1967, 1969); Bianca Maria Pagani, *L'emigrazione friulana della metà del secolo XIX al 1940* (Udine, 1968); Luigi Ridolfi, *I friulani nell'Argentina* (Udine, 1949).

nia, and Russia. By the time the great Friulan movement to North America began (after 1900) migration was so much a part of the culture of the region that in many towns remaining at home was a sign of deviance. A 1928 article in the Milan daily, *Corriere della Sera*, wrote of the piedmont in Friuli as a region where "it is easier for one to go to New York rather than to Genoa or Naples. Here, it certainly seems simpler to leave for Poland or Canada than for Udine, the capital city of the region. Under the small porticos everyone speaks about Paris, Warsaw, Budapest, and Vienna as if they were located nearby."[2] Temporary migration has been an integral part of the Friulan economy for many generations. The region is divided into gravel flatlands and a coastal area in the south, a piedmont in the center and a barren mountainous zone in the north. It was from the infertile north that some of the earliest sojourners left the region. Silk and linen weavers from Carnia peddled their skills across Europe by the mid-sixteenth century.[3] However, it was when machinery replaced the Carnian textile workers in the mid-nineteenth century that the great *Auswanderung* began from Udine. Industrialization and the increasing activity in the public works sector in the form of decorative buildings, railways, and monuments created an enormous demand for building tradesmen and laborers all across Europe.

An emigration commissioner in Udine, Giovanni Cosattini, traced the eastward movement of the Friulan tradesmen:

> From Austria they moved into Germany, from there in 1875 into Hungary, then in 1876 down into Bosnia, Rumania and Bulgaria and finally Serbia; now they go to Russia, Siberia, Turkey and Asia Minor, tomorrow to China and the Transvaal.[4]

The dimensions of these temporary migrations were indeed remarkable. In 1901 Friuli accounted for 49,448 temporary migrants, or 80.5 per 1,000 population (including urban areas). Venetia, with a total of 111,758 temporary migrants (the highest in the country), was the only other region to approach that rate, with 35 migrants per 1,000. The rest of the peninsula averaged only 5.71 per 1,000. But these figures reveal little about the situation in individual towns. Resia

---

[2] O. Vergani, "Il miracolo millenario del mosaico," *Corriere dell Sera*, 20 April 1928, p. 6.

[3] Giovanni Cosattini, "L'emigrazione temporanea del Friuli," *Bollettino dell' emigrazione* no. 3 (Rome, 1904), pp. 14–15.

[4] Ibid., p. 17.

(Moggio) in Carnia recorded 1,638 migrants out of a town population of 3,952, while Magnano in Riviera recorded 808 out of 2,573, rates of 41.45 percent and 31.4 percent, respectively.[5] In these towns and others, where virtually all fit men began the annual pilgrimage in February, March, or April, the family economy—indeed, the family cycle itself—revolved around the migration experience. Grandparents, wives, and children worked the farm and fattened the livestock that would be slaughtered in December when the father returned with the season's savings—often to sire another child. Little wonder that Cosattini remarked that "for our people emigration has by now [1904] become a necessity, a profession. If a foreign country no longer has employment opportunities for *Friulani*, we will have to look elsewhere." As a nineteenth-century liberal, Cosattini neither condemned nor condoned such large-scale movements of population. Even though he lamented that sojourning had given Udine the dubious distinction of recording the highest rate of syphilitic deaths in Italy in 1896, he saw emigration as a natural phenomenon that could not, and should not, be halted.[6]

Three major occupations emerged for Friulan migrants during the eighteenth and nineteenth centuries: 1) the fine building trades—mosaics, marble, tile, and terrazzo; 2) other building trades—brick making, stonecutting, and general labor in buildings, quarries, and on railway lines; and 3) bricklaying. A fourth occupation of some significance was woodcutting. Perhaps this migration of skilled labor can best be understood by tracing some of the occupational groups from Friuli through Europe, and ultimately to towns and cities in North America.

Although most Friulan emigrants were in the rough trades, they were particularly identified with mosaics, marble, tile, and terrazzo work. Luigi Ridolfi, a steamship chaplain who recorded his visits to dozens of Friulan settlements in North America in two books, reported that "when one wishes to find *Friulani* in a city, one must find out if there are terrazzo and mosaic companies and then approach them. Often the contractor is American but the employees are *Friu-*

---

[5] Ibid., pp. 18–21. Excellent statistics on emigration and destinations of each hometown are available for the 1880s and 1890s in annual reports from Min. di Agricoltura, Industria e Commercio, Dir. Gen. della Statistica, *Statistica della emigrazione italiana* (Rome).

[6] Cosattini, "L'emigrazione temporanea," pp. 89, 93.

lani .... The exception is Canada, where bricklayers, miners, and factory laborers preceded terrazzo and mosaic workers."[7] The mosaic tradesmen were almost exclusively from Spilimbergo and two nearby towns, Fanna and Sequals. At about the age of ten, boys in this area began the two-year course at the famous mosaic school in Spilimbergo. After graduating, they were expected to apprentice with a contractor and begin the life of a sojourner.

Friulani began to export their trade to Venice around the turn of the nineteenth century and by 1825 they were established in France. The migration to that country expanded, especially after 1850, when the *mosaicisti* were found in significant numbers in Montpellier, Beziers, and Nimes. They subsequently diffused their trade throughout Europe. One filiopietistic student of migration, Ludovico Zanini, wrote short biographies of the great terrazzo and mosaic contractors. A list of them illustrates the eastward movement of the trade— Giandomenico Facchina in Paris in the 1850s (the mosaics of the Opera were his masterpiece); Giovanni Odorico from Sequals in Vienna, Berlin, Dresden, Frankfurt, and Amsterdam; Vincenzo Odorico in Copenhagen; and Ermengildo Cristofori from Sequals and his hundreds of employees in Budapest and in the provinces of Moscow, Nizhnii Novgorod, and Kazan in Russia.[8] The contractors sent artisans to other urban centers to affix precut and set mosaics. If these employees saw a possible market, they often remained in the city to begin their own businesses. The first Friulan mosaic company in North America, Ideal Mosaic Company, began precisely in that manner. Giandomenico Facchina of Paris sent two employees to New York City in 1880 to work on the mosaics of the Vanderbilt mansion, and the two men—from Busceglia and Sequals—decided to stay.[9]

This process was repeated throughout the North American continent. When the Despirt family of Buffalo sent employee Albino Pedron to Toronto in 1915, he established the Art Mosaic and Ter-

[7] Luigi Ridolfi, *I Friulani nell'America del Nord* (Udine, 1931), p. 43. Ridolfi wrote two other books on the *Friulani* in North America. *Quadri e cuori* (Udine, 1947) is a short account of Friulan settlements on the continent. *Lacrime cristiane* (Udine, 1952) is a historical novel dealing with a terrazzo worker who cuts off relations with his family and abandons his Catholic faith to become a communist; he then returns to the faith, establishes contact with his family, and travels through Friulan settlements in North America counseling other wayward migrants to do the same.
[8] Zanini, *Friuli migrante*, pp. 151 ff.
[9] Ridolfi, *Friulani nell'America del Nord*, pp. 17–19.

razzo Company. From Buffalo, the Despirts did the work for the Cook County Courthouse in Chicago, the pre-1906 San Francisco Post Office, and Toronto General Hospital.[10] Mosaic and terrazzo contractors eventually settled in each of those cities; in fact, after Pedron began his business in Toronto, one of the Despirt sons opened a satellite firm for the family in the growing Ontario city.[11] From Toronto, the Despirts and Pedron sent employees to Ottawa, Hamilton, Timmins, Sudbury, Montreal, Halifax, and other cities. Their employees eventually formed their own companies in each of these towns (another Despirt opened a Montreal branch). The Friulan mosaic workers diffused their trade throughout North America between 1900 and 1903, just as they had done in Europe fifty years earlier. By 1930 contractors from Fanna were operating in Atlanta, Chattanooga, Schenectady, and St. Louis, and in Jackson and Battle Creek, Michigan. One man from Travesio owned the Terrazzo and Mosaic Company of Tulsa, Oklahoma, and two partners from Sequals ran a firm in Montgomery, Alabama. Contractors also brought the trade to Ann Arbor, Michigan, and Sioux City, Iowa. The De Marco family (originally from Maniago) in Omaha sent employees to Missouri, Kansas, Colorado, Nebraska, and Louisiana.[12]

Luigi Ridolfi was as filiopietistic toward North American contractors as Zanini was toward European entrepreneurs. Ridolfi referred to some of them as patriarchs of the mosaic trade, and he ascribed a civilizing role to these artisans. When he noticed their absence in Gary, Indiana, he observed, "Our *Friulani*, in their characteristic role of mosaic pioneers, have not yet come to Gary: perhaps the city is too young and not developed enough to appreciate the treasures of museum art . . . . The great names of Sequals, Cavasso Nuovo and Fanna, true factories of terrazzo and mosaics, are missing. They can be found, instead, in the state capital, Indianapolis."[13] Ridolfi noticed that there were few *Friulani* in Sacramento and in the American West in general: "It will take a great deal for the West to match the American East. But it will not be long before the American standard of living will be equalized throughout the country and so our *Friulani*,

[10] Mary Forbes (Albino Pedron's daughter), interview with author, 27 March 1979.

[11] Gid De Spirt, interview with author, 1 October 1980.

[12] Ridolfi, *Friulani nell'America del Nord*, pp. 44–60.

[13] Ibid., p. 49.

with their American rapid grinders, will also flourish."[14] These artisans in search of markets combed the continent and made their trade
almost synonymous with Friulan migration.

Numerically, brick makers ranked behind the mosaic workers and
builders among Friulan immigrants, but the recent romanticization
of their brazen manners and attitudes perhaps have made them the
most popular of temporary migrants from the region. Every spring,
10,000 to 15,000 men over the age of ten traveled to more than 200
brick ovens in rural Bavaria. A subcontractor (*accordante*) hired men
(hundreds of whom lived in the town of Buia alone) during the late
winter. In the spring they followed him to the villages surrounding
Munich to work as brick molders (*formatori* or *stampatori*), glazers
(*fuochiati* or *fornaciai*), or in some cases general laborers.

The *fornaciai* (the generic term for anyone involved in brick making), who were primarily from the plains of Udine, were described by
one writer as "among the most uncouth [*rozzi*] and least educated
peasants."[15] Zanini attributed the replacement of German, Austrian,
Bohemian, and Tyrolean brick makers by *Friulani* to their ability to
work outdoors in the heat of the sun and to survive on an inexpensive diet of cornmeal (*polenta*) with virtually no meat.[16] In addition,
the *Friulani* introduced the use of soft clay and a method of drying
bricks flat on the ground rather than upright—two efficient innova-
tions. Brick making as a Friulan occupation did not spread far beyond Bavaria, except in Argentina. However, one entrepreneur named
Fuoraboschi, who ran a forestry firm in Bosnia, opened a brick factory in Irkutsk (Siberia) in 1903. A significant number of *fornaciai*,
especially those from Zompicchia (Codroipo), worked for Canadian
firms on the outskirts of Toronto—in Mimico, Milton, Port Credit,
New Toronto, Cooksville, and in the East End of Toronto.[17]

If the trade itself did not spread, most of the *Friulani* who worked
in the Bavarian brick factories certainly made their way around the
world. For many migrants, work in the brick ovens was a stepping-

---

[14] Ibid., p. 67.

[15] Giacomo Pertile, "Gli italiani in Germania," *Bollettino dell'emigrazione* no.
11 (Rome, 1914), p. 103. Another excellent study on the brick makers is P. Sandic-
chi's "I fornaciai in Baviera," *Bollettino dell'emigrazione* no. 12 (Rome, 1912), pp.
3–40.

[16] Zanini, *Friuli migrante*, pp. 215–16.

[17] Albina de Clare, interview with author, 9 March 1980; Luigi Piccoli, interview
with author, 23 May 1980.

stone to other traditional occupations. Cosattini noted:

> Young boys ordinarily begin their long odyssey in the brick factories
> (*fornaci*), which are for them a first experiment, a dolorous attempt at
> withstanding the fatigue, privations, and the pain which must be faced
> in life. After a year or two they abandon the brick factory and they
> become employed as laborers and bricklayers' apprentices, carrying
> masonry and bricks, almost as if attracted to this work by an atavistic
> passion; following this, they work on rough brick and stone projects,
> and with time, if they have intelligence and ingenuity they take on
> some finer cement projects, ornamental work, moldings.[18]

On one level, then, mosaic, marble, and terrazzo works; bricklaying
and stonecutting; and brick making were three separate employment
paths, but on another level they formed one broad Friulan migrant
occupational category—the skilled and semiskilled building trades.
Ridolfi himself implicitly recognized this; he often used the word *im-
presario* (contractor) with no qualifying adjective. In other words, it
did not matter whether the person was a bricklaying, marble, carpen-
try, or general contractor—he was a building contractor.

Friulani in nonmosaic building trades and those in mining, forestry,
and peddling were dispersed throughout North America, partly as
a response to American needs, but also as a result of the previous
Friulan migrations in Europe. The most notable aspect of any Friulan
migrant occupation was its mobility or flexibility—an ability to adapt
to all environments. A *scalpellino* or *tagliapietra* (stonecutter) could
be found working in the quarries of Rumania in 1900, building a
tunnel for the trans-Siberian railway in the Baikal in the 1890s, or
repairing tracks for the Canadian Pacific Railway at the turn of the
century.

Cosattini saw nothing remarkable in the mobility of those involved
in the building trades. He perceived correctly that Friulan stonecutters and bricklayers were simply attempting to maximize cash returns
for their skills. He observed that *Friulani* in search of high salaries did
not choose countries or regions with large, organized proletariats, but
rather sought those areas where no indigenous group worked in the
construction field:

> Thus, for example, in the construction of the Damascus-Mecca railway
> many *Friulani* were employed as assistants, bricklayers and stonema-
> sons and firemen at the rate of one *Friulano* for every two Arabs. The

---

[18] Cosattini, "L'emigrazione temporanea," p. 46.

latter had no knowledge of the art of solid construction required for the project. The salaries were therefore very high.[19]

For the same reason, a group of *Friulani* followed Leonard Perini of Artenia to the Caucasus between 1876 and 1880 to construct thirteen pylons across the Volga for a railway bridge. In the 1890s, ninety men from the town of Clausetto followed Pietro Brovedan, a contractor from their town, to work on the tunnels of the trans-Siberian railway between Obi and Irkutsk.[20] At the same time, bricklayers and stonemasons from Portis and Venzone went off to work for the Rumanian contractors Simon and Mincu.[21] A group of stonecutters came to Montreal in 1904 to work on the Canadian Pacific Railway tracks in the Canadian north.[22] Friulan migration to North America was very much a product of North American occupational demands and conditions and earlier Friulan sojourning traditions. We have already seen how terrazzo workers, bricklayers, and stonemasons saw North America as an extension of European markets. The woodsmen from eastern Friuli who worked around Tacoma, Washington, or in northern Ontario were continuing to practice a skill for which *Friulani* were well known in western Rumania. Perhaps Andrea de Gleria, who in 1930 owned a cutlery shop in Seattle, was among the last of the Friulan peddlers to hawk knives from Maniago across Europe, Asia, and North America.[23] One can even make a case that to some extent mining and railway labor used some of the skills required for

---

[19] Ibid., pp. 47–48.

[20] Salvatore Minocchi, "Gli italiani nel Caucaso, in Siberia e in Manciuria," *Bollettino dell'emigrazione* no. 6 (Rome, 1905), pp. 8–13. See also his "Gli italiani in Siberia e in Manciuria," *Rassegna Nazionale* 147 (1904): 181–98.

[21] Zanini, *Friuli migrante*, p. 96.

[22] The CPR labor agent, Antonio Cordasco, wrote to Udine steamship agent Antonio Paretti: "Many of your men declare that they are stonecutters, and that you promised them I would have them employed in this quality. I never wrote this." Cordasco to Paretti, 26 April 1904. See Canada Department of Labour, Sessional Paper 36b, *The Royal Commission Appointed to Inquire into the Immigration of Italian Labourers to Montreal and the Alleged Fraudulent Practices of Employment Agencies* (Ottawa, 1905), p. 82.

[23] Ridolfi, *Friulani nell'America del Nord*, pp. 68–69. Cosattini noted that in 1904 Friuli had 447 *girovaghi* (itinerant migrants), including knife peddlers: "Almost all of the products of the region's cutlery firms (240 small manufactories) are sold by peddlers from the respective towns, who are dispersed throughout the world." The *girovaghi* also included some knife grinders, pot and pan vendors, and the salami peddlers from Gemona and Tarcento who operated in Vienna. See Cosattini, "L'emigrazione temporanea," pp. 61–62, 13.

stonecutting. But new opportunities for employment in industry, especially in Canada, brought *Friulani* to the pulp and paper plants in Powell River and the smelter in Trail, British Columbia, and to the huge steel factories of Sault Ste. Marie and Hamilton, Ontario. If occupations in heavy industry and mining did have a link with traditional Friulan migration it was in the manner in which they were dispersed throughout the North American continent. As in Europe, by 1930 Friulan migrants had settled in large cities, small towns, and in mining, industrial, and rural communities. Unlike most Italian immigrants they were not exclusively urban settlers. In 1931 when Luigi Ridolfi published his memoirs of travel through Friulan communities in North America, he calculated that 12,200 *Friulani* lived in North America—9,000 in the United States and 3,200 in Canada. They lived in six provinces and forty-two states. "[In Canada] the majority are in the mines and factories; a large part are bricklayers and stonemasons and terrazzo workers; a few others are brick makers and laborers." However, on the continent as a whole the *Friulani* were most prominent as terrazzo and mosaic workers, then as *muratori* (including laborers), as industrial workers and miners, and finally as brick makers and farmers—occupations that could be adapted to any part of the continent.[24]

Ridolfi found his *paesani* in all major and medium-sized cities and in numerous small towns. He recorded 230 *Friulani* in the smelting town of Trail and a few in Cranbrooke and Fernie, British Columbia. *Friulani* were in the coal mining towns of Natal, Michel, Rossland, Corbin, White Sulphur, Revelstoke, and Crowsnest, British Columbia; and in Mountain Park, Venice, Coleman, Blairmore, Bellevue, Coalhurst, Maple Leaf, Lethbridge, Taber, and Turner Valley, Alberta. In the metal mining region of northern Ontario, Conniston had twelve families and Creighton Mines had two families. *Friulani* also lived and worked in Kirkland Lake, Trout Lake, Sudbury, Copper Cliff, Timmins, Cobalt, Cochrane, Porcupine, Levack, and Huntsville, Ontario. Ridolfi wrote proudly about the *Friulano* in Garson Mine who owned a gold mine and about the two gold prospectors from Zompicchia and Zoppola who worked on the British Columbia–Alaska border.

In the United States, Ridolfi found small pockets of *Friulani* around New York City—in New Rochelle, Mount Vernon, White Plains, Tor-

---

[24] Ridolfi, *Friulani nell'America del Nord*, p. 147.

rington and Corona; and on the Buffalo-Boston route—in Rochester, Syracuse, Utica, Albany, and Berlin. Even Salem, Massachusetts, had one family, and nearby Beverly had two. Pennsylvania also hosted small groups—in Butler, Greensburg, Midland, Scranton, and New Salem. Each of these towns was the destination of one or two sending towns in Friuli.

Friulani were usually found in small groups. In fact, when Ridolfi could name only a few immigrants and their sending towns in some of the mining communities of the Crowsnest Pass in western Canada, he assured readers, "I do not believe they are the only ones, because *Friulani* like to stay in groups. Ordinarily an immigrant has a bad start when he isolates himself from friends and acquaintances." However, he saw nothing wrong with the thirty or so single migrants in Fernie, British Columbia, who boarded with *connazionali*, that is, with Italians rather than *Friulani*, or with the *Friulani* of Sault Ste. Marie who lived together "with the large Italian colony." But he was totally baffled when, in Victoria, British Columbia, "in a true maze of shacks in an entirely Chinese quarter ... I marveled to find some *Friulani*."[25]

Although the *Friulani* were dispersed throughout the continent, their emigration to each settlement was not random. Each town in Friuli had its own migration targets, although some men, the so-called prodigal migrants, chose new destinations and lost contact with home. The Friulan experience in North America is an excellent example of how a regional group in the Old World cultivated particular skills and chose specific destination points for its prospective migrants. From the earliest days, the Friulan builders found a niche in the building programs of the great cities: Haussmann's Paris projects, the Ringstrasse in Vienna, and Fifth Avenue mansions in New York were the settings for the early generations of migrants. But as the labor market of Friulan builders grew, so did the work opportunities, especially in North America. Mosaic and terrazzo in civic buildings became symbols of great-city status all across the United States and Canada. In that sense, the migrants from Friuli were not only skilled tradesmen in search of opportunity, but also purveyors of urban culture.

---

[25] Ibid., p. 73.

Small Town
Little Italies

Italian Folk Culture Transplanted: Methods of Documentation

Carla Bianco

A wave of change has swept through most traditional cultures. In particular, the so-called folk cultures of the past, which produced the distinctive characteristics of ethnic and regional identities, are now undergoing processes of change whose most visible effect seems to be the spread of a leveling and dull uniformity. Worried observers with different concerns—political, philosophical, artistic—have tried to identify the causes of that process and to propose possible anti-dotes. The possibility of salvaging what remains of traditional cultures, or of reviving from the past some selected aspects of an almost vanished tradition, has been discussed. While I have tried to contribute to this debate on other occasions, I mention it here only to explain how I first became interested in the study of Italian peasant emigration. A thorough study of this complex phenomenon would certainly require interdisciplinary competence, but a global approach was never in my plans, as I was only interested in some cultural consequences of that phenomenon.

I began with the assumption that the leveling forces—which I do not present here as either positive or negative—are likely to produce differing effects depending on the social position and class of the groups that become exposed to them. Using comparative methods and considering as equivalent the concepts of folk culture and peasant culture, I wanted to find out what had happened to Italian folk traditions in the United States and Canada two or three generations after massive immigration. I wanted to discover which aspects of the traditional culture had been most influenced by the acculturating power of urban and industrial America and whether the changes had been mostly in the direction of an increasing loss of cultural diversity and hence toward assimilation and uniformity. The immigrants had come from an agricultural-pastoral context; since time immemorial their worldview, their working skills, and the form of their social organization had been molded by the requirements of that past experience. Going to America necessarily meant a radical change of both physical and social conditions, but those peasant ideas and practices—the only cultural "baggage" the immigrants brought—were for a long time the immigrants' only points of reference in their interaction with the new reality.

My initial interest in this subject was stimulated by the marks emigration left on Italian peasant culture at home—on the kinship relationships, on oral literature, on material culture, and on the general worldview. In the early sixties, one could hardly visit an Italian village without meeting at least a few of the so-called *Americani*, returned migrants still holding an old American passport and even an American pension. I realized that practically all of the informants I was contacting in my field trips in southern and central Italy had been affected by emigration, each having at least a few relatives in the United States, in Canada, or elsewhere. I consider emigration an "evidencer" of cultural phenomena; the cultural processes that can be observed in immigrant life offer insights for anthropological research that are not easily seen under conditions of residential stability and continuity.

The conceptual frame of reference I chose for my study was the assumption that the acculturation of folklore (i.e., traditional peasant culture) depended on two main variables: the varying amount of pressure for assimilation from the host society; and the economic and social role of the individual or the group within the structure of the new society. Within this framework, I wanted to examine the function of folklore in the immigrant's life and the extent to which traditional views coexisted, syncretically, with the acquisition of new cultural and social ways. In particular, I hoped to understand whether the cognitive organization of the peasant culture could reestablish internal coherence after blending with the new cultural patterns, or whether the folkloric basis of the immigrant culture clashed with the new situation and became subordinate. In the latter case, the result might have been a mass of heterogeneous, unsystematic, and conflictual information—a sort of cultural entropy—and I expected to find its lasting evidence in the present folkways of the group.

A major problem of my study was the lack at that time of models in existing research. Apart from limited historical research and a vast literature on folk revival, little anthropological study of the problems presented here is available. This paper consists of a brief account of my research design and findings, along with comments on choices, dilemmas, and mistakes. It is, in other words, the translation of theoretical concerns into an operative design.

The Roseto Study: Aims and Methods

Between 1962 and 1964, I collected data, first in the Italian areas of departure, second in the corresponding places of settlement in the United States. This procedure, which allowed me to follow village and kinship ties, provided the basis for a comparative analysis because it involved fairly homogeneous groups. In addition, it offered an easy introduction to the Italian American people. I discovered how pleased my American informants were when I showed photographs and played taped messages collected from their relatives in Italy. My firsthand knowledge of the folk culture of the villages of origin proved to be a useful orientation for field research among the American descendants. The first year was spent collecting material in several Italian American settlements of different regional origin. This first phase served as a methodological training for the formulation of the subsequent study of a single group. In 1964 I discovered Roseto, Pennsylvania, because of the sudden attention this little town had received in the international press. A team of specialists in genetics and heart disease from the Oklahoma Medical School had found an unusually low rate of heart attacks and a long life span in Roseto, despite the high caloric intake and widespread obesity there. Roseto seemed perfect for my study. This small industrial town of about 2,000 inhabitants (95 percent of whom were descendants of the same village in Italy: Roseto Valfortore, Foggia) presented nearly ideal observational conditions. Its size, equal to that of its Italian counterpart, allowed easy control of various aspects of lifestyle. Its economy made the experience of this community fairly representative of that of the Italian American group at large, as it underwent a radical change from an agricultural to an industrial identity. Its demographic homogeneity appeared particularly suitable for a comparative study with the Italian Roseto. Finally, the close contacts with the neighboring groups (Welsh, English, and German, as well as Neapolitan, Abruzzese, Marchigiano, Veneto, etc.) in this community also resembled the Italian American experience at large and permitted the observation of interethnic behavior.

Although the Roseto study was based on a comparative approach, I did not want a flat comparison of the two towns—a sort of "Roseto here and Roseto there." I was mainly interested in the American Roseto, which I saw as a privileged angle of observation for studying the results of a process. However, since that process had started from the Italian Roseto, where its consequences were still observable, I decided that both diachronic and synchronic perspectives could be secured by first spending a few months in the village of origin. Only with an acceptable knowledge of the culture of that village could I begin my research in the immigrant community. The experience I had previously acquired in my pilot survey of other Italian groups clearly indicated that this procedure was the correct—though time-consuming—one.

A large part of my field data consisted of folk traditions, that is, the traditional practices and ideas about most aspects of life—kinship, health and nutrition, sex, education, religion, entertainment, work, and other social activities and relationships. In other words, folk traditions are those cultural aspects less characterized by the patterns of the official society and mostly—though not solely—inherited from the Italian peasant tradition. In this part of the inquiry, I chose to avoid the antiquarian approach of relic collecting and also the neopopulist streams of revivalism. Consequently, there was no triumph in finding folk beliefs and practices still alive among the American Rosetans, nor were there tears for each piece of the ancestral culture "lost" by the informants. I simply regarded syncretism, substitution, and maintenance as a part of the obvious process of acculturation that all cultural minorities go through when their social experience and geographical setting have been radically changed. My goal was to identify some of the factors at work in the manifold process of culture change, as well as to find possible determinants of culture maintenance.

I supplemented the scanty and heterogeneous literature existing on the two Rosetos by collecting oral histories in both towns, as well as by assembling materials such as genealogies, photographs, newspapers, letters, domestic account books, and administrative and political records. A special type of diachronic dimension was obtained by comparing the same items of folklore—songs, magic spells, folktales—from both towns, as well as from Rosetans contacted in Canada. I decided to organize my investigation around thematic sectors that categorized the most important aspects of life. These include the physical setting, social life (work, family, recreational activities), and ceremonial life. I do not pretend to establish a classification of human activities, and the methods presented here are certainly not the only possible ones.

The Setting

My study included data on the Roseto setting. By setting, I mean the culturally prescribed residential patterns and concepts of space—both private and public. Particular attention was given to: 1) the overall structure and organization of town space—the network of streets, squares, churches, public buildings, and shops; 2) the form, orientation, and building criteria of the houses; 3) criteria of structural distribution and actual use of internal space—number and type of rooms, patterns of furnishing, patterns of sex, age, and other social divisions of space; 4) residential organization among kin—proximity of dwellings and past and present patrilocal and matrilocal tendencies; and 5) the relationship between residential and working space.

One of the most interesting findings that emerged from the data on setting was that the persistence of traditional modalities is almost exclusively limited to the use of the material structures. The structures themselves only rarely reveal an identifiable Italian style. While this situation is basically true for all of North America (and for most other places of Italian immigration), it is especially significant that it should characterize Roseto, a town founded, built, inhabited, and administered solely by the descendants of the same Italian village. Apart from the Catholic church (dedicated, as in Italy, to "Our

Lady of Mt. Carmel," or *la Madonna del Carmine*), which shows some Romanesque influence, all Rosetan buildings follow the stylistic and structural patterns firmly established all over North America long before the Italian immigration. In spite of the fact that both recently and in the past most Rosetans built their houses with their own hands, none recall the Italian formal elements that were certainly familiar to the immigrants. There are at least three main reasons for this widespread trend: 1) the widely established central and northern European patterns (both ideal and material) in the public sectors of life; 2) a conscious or unconscious effort to remove the visible features that reveal one's own peasant origins; and 3) the dynamics of material culture, which usually imply a more rapid and radical change of forms and techniques with respect to other aspects of culture.

Material culture depends on such conditioning factors as raw materials (e.g., the abundance of wood versus the scarcity of stone or marble), laws, and market pressures. Consequently, the building patterns and techniques—and also such items as furniture, clothing, and utensils—were exposed to a quick and radical process of loss and substitution. However, the use of the material structures still shows, after two or three generations, a strong traditional orientation. The term "use" refers to a number of different aspects, from the names attributed to streets and public buildings (Garibaldi, Colombo, Dante, Pio XI) to the actual purpose of such spaces as squares, front porches, backyards, kitchens, lounges, basements, and even windows and doorways. The latter are a good example of what is meant here. Far from being merely passages and openings for people, air, and light, they also serve the very important function—essential in a traditional society—of mutual social control. An open doorway is an open contact with the community, an open contact that is expected by the social mores of the group, which call for interpersonal and reciprocal inspection. The common American "right to privacy," on the other hand, requires providing everyone a screen against intrusion.

Social Life

Work. The emigration experience has always revolved around the central issue of work; the emigrant's survival in America depended on his working abilities. However, the specific skills that characterized the majority of Italian peasants on arrival in America were agricultural

Evil eye ceremony in Roseto, Pennsylvania, 1966.
Photo courtesy of Carla Bianco.

or pastoral in nature; they included those minor arts and crafts associated with traditional agricultural systems and societies—cobbling, potting, blacksmithing. These skills could only rarely find application in the urban and industrial areas of settlement in America; the documented cases of reapplication of such activities as marble carver, potter, fisherman, or shepherd are exceptions to the general trends. On the other hand, the modernization of American agriculture at the time of Italian immigration posed a severe challenge for the Italian peasant, owing to the experience he possessed from his past relationship with the land and its cultivation (subsistence economy, feudal work relationships, archaic technology, village residential patterns). Consequently, the traditional working skills, as well as concepts of work and of its purposes, survived only in the restricted context of the domestic sphere of life (house and garden), and self-employment based on small, individual enterprise (barber, tailor, baker, fruit vendor, butcher, shoemaker, etc.). In industrial and other productive activities, the acknowledged working skills of the immigrant were largely limited to a great determination, inventiveness, endurance, and muscular strength. My research data confirm the pattern; the majority of my informants were labeled as "unskilled labor" for a long time, although they had been, and still were at the time of immigration, the carriers of ancient and respected skills handed down from father to son for the survival of the peasant society. Thus, while they appeared totally unskilled for the public sector of life, they continued to apply their traditional knowledge to the private and self-directed sectors. The life histories I collected, an invaluable source for this type of investigation, all confirm this trend. The field data cover a wide variety of materials, including biographical narratives, old and recent photographs of working situations, lengthy descriptions of various techniques (cooking, sewing, wine making, gardening, canning, fishing, etc.), and even tools and some finished products, such as carved and woven objects.

Family and kinship. The 47 "migratory genealogies" in my collection show that the migratory experience has made the peasant family the most dismembered aspect of traditional culture: "La carne nostra sta a tutti i pizzi" (our flesh is scattered all over the world) is the recurrent commentary I heard while collecting genealogical data. Each family has close relatives in distant lands: Australia, Canada, England, Italy, Brazil, France, Argentina, Venezuela, Germany, Switzerland, and Belgium, in addition to the numerous settlements in the United States. Partly as a reaction to the abrupt separation at the time of emigration, and partly because of the need for reciprocal support in facing the difficulties of the new life, family cohesion and kinship ties and loyalties often acquired a new strength, at least during the first years of adjustment. Today, in spite of the deep changes which have clearly transformed the Italo-American family, one can easily see the survival of the traditional Italian kinship system. In other words, it is possible to see how the kinship network still functions as a social bulwark and as a kind of separate social universe. Compared to Americans of central or northern European origin, the modern descendants of the Italian immigrants still confine a significant part of their social relationships to their kinship network, especially in connection with certain crucial moments of the life cycle, such as sickness, birth, marriage, and death.

In addition to using the genealogical method, I studied kinship patterns through intensive participant observation, as well as by collecting data from private and public archives (e.g., family scrapbooks, diaries, letters, wills). I was interested in: 1) the size of the kinship range of knowledge of each informant; 2) the type and level of economic cooperation among kin; 3) the organizational and/or normative character of kin groups; 4) the form and the quantity of contacts with relatives living abroad; 5) ideas about and practice of a system of obligation among kin in various life situations; and 6) kinship terminology, both in Italian and in English. I also collected many proverbs and traditional anecdotes about family and kinship relationships, letters, and information on attendance at special family gatherings and celebrations.

Recreational and associational activities. Deep changes are obvious in this sector of life, which includes family and public gatherings for recreational activities (e.g., dances, games, storytelling and singing sessions, sports), patterns of social visiting (Sunday family gatherings), and club attendance (Marconi Social Club, city bands). Most of these activities are acquiring—or have already acquired—the form and content that characterize the social life of industrial and urban America today. But in spite of this obvious and immediately visible process of assimilation, certain traditional forms are still practiced, although in modified versions, with new functions, and in changed occasions with respect to the original system of folkways.

In other words, with respect to the living conditions that originally produced them, these associative and recreational forms often appear as authentic "survivals" in the evolutionistic sense of the term, that is, without the social functions they used to have, or even with no function at all. But a closer look at the total social life of the group reveals that these forms have an orientative function important for the support of the group identity and cohesion.

As already indicated, the range of formal and informal social activities rather artificially grouped in this section is extremely large and heterogeneous; therefore, I made a special effort to keep the data firmly organized within the same frame of variables used for the rest of the inquiry: sex, age, social class, occupation, time spent in America, area of settlement. For the most part, however, these extremely varied data do show some regularities; the most relevant one in my opinion is the strong tendency of the Italian-born and the first American-born generations to perform 75 to 93 percent of the activities represented in this section within the kinship and neighborhood context. The percentage diminishes with the second American-born generation, which shows a tendency to perform only 30 to 37 percent of such activities within family and kinship circles and which shows very little interest in the neighborhood context.

The public sector of life. It is not easy—or even possible—to find a scientific justification for a category such as "public life," since all the aspects included in the other sections of this framework also occur in public to some extent. I am not happy, therefore, with this heading, although I found it necessary in my fieldwork to have a tentative category that would allow me to organize my observations of those informants' behaviors and ideas that refer to the changing concepts of "public" and "private." In general, the recurrent pattern of syncretic combination of the two concepts, in both their traditional and their modern American senses, dominated attitudes toward educational, political, and economic life. This is why I assembled under this heading such themes as school, press, politics, and patriotic manifestations. It seems to me that the data I was able to assemble are particularly revealing of the particular state of "suspension" between a traditional group identity and the ways of American society. However, it is also evident that the actual possibility of identifying this syncretic and often conflictual situation as it refers to attitudes toward the public sphere of life must be methodologically linked to a comparative analysis of the overall traditional worldview examined in the other sections.

Ceremonial Life

Naturally, a number of important correlations can be established between the ceremonies accompanying the critical moments of an individual's life and his or her relationship with the kinship network. Data from both Italy and the United States once again show the general trend by which the rites connected with life-cycle events—such as birth, marriage, and death—are largely celebrated with relatives. In fact, I believe that the survival of traditional rites and ceremonies and of the corresponding system of ideas and beliefs is partly due to a sort of symbiotic relationship. Ritual and ceremonial life functioned and survived with the protection and support offered by the kinship system, which in turn was allowed to continue in most of its traditional forms thanks to the ritualization of kinship bonds and functions. I do not wish to reduce the structural correlation between the ceremonial and the kinship systems to the level of the well-known puzzle of which came first: the chicken or the egg. I would simply stress the importance of mutual dependence of these two systems within the context of the acculturative process. While the immigrants struggled with the dilemmas presented by the new society, they could continue to rely on those two systems by following their traditional views. A discussion of the social and psychological factors of the continuity of ceremonial life also involves study of the causal relationship between that continuity and the economic and social history of the immigrants. In anthropological terms, that is the relationship between social life and worldview.

With regard to documentation—the subject of this paper—I can say that this section is one of the best documented in my collection. It includes a large quantity and variety of materials: photographs; taped interviews about magic and religious practice and belief (black magic, miracles, folk medicine, etc.); ritual objects (the "Only True Letter of Jesus Christ," scapulars, religious broadsides, prayer books, and amulets); oral traditions (legends and songs); newspapers; and other printed materials. Field observation and interviewing were largely organized around the two "tool" concepts of "life cycle" and "year cycle" (Van Gennep, 1909), while other categories, such as that of "folklore genre" (Ben Amos, 1976), were also used whenever the concept of "rites of passage" could not be applied. Always, I followed the theoretical rule of examining ritual and ceremonial behavior in close correlation with the rest of the life experience (Vecoli, 1977), my purpose being to avoid the irrational positions that ignore the existence of such causal correlations.

Conclusions

The documentation of all three sections provides glimpses of the difficult and uneven history of contacts between the two related groups across the Atlantic Ocean and, also, among the relatives scattered all over the world by emigration. For more than a hundred years, millions of Italians have been involved in an unending pilgrimage, from one country to another, in a permanent state of spatial and cultural suspension. The oral accounts of the informants tell of endless journeys—by ship, by train, on foot, legally and illegally—to reach a port of embarkation, or to move to still another country, in search of a better job and to reach long-dreamed-of conditions, or to escape from no longer acceptable ones; to go back home, or to go away forever, in anger and desperation, as in the emigration ballad:

> Io parto per l'America / sul lungo bastimento,
> parto col cuor contento / di non vederti più.
> (I leave for America / I sail on the long steamship,
> My heart is happy / for I shall see you no more.)

In conclusion, mine was not a nostalgic search for the relics of a dismembered Italian heritage abroad, nor a romantic celebration of the supposedly unique qualities and longevity of that heritage, nor a saga-like recitation of the pains suffered, the risks afforded, and the victories gained by our emigrants. My aim was to investigate the dynamics of the acculturative process, by means of comparative research methods applied to a migrating culture. If I have succeeded in at least introducing the problem from the point of view of a possible mode of research, I shall be satisfied.

References
Ben Amos, Dan. *Folklore Genres.* Austin, 1976.
Bianco, Carla. *Italian and Italian-American Folklore: A Working Bibliography.* Folklore Forum, no. 5. Bloomington, 1970.
————. *The Two Rosetos.* Bloomington, 1974.

_____. *Emigrazione: Processi di acculturazione in Canada e negli Stati Uniti*. Bari, 1980.

_____. "Ethnicism and Culturology: The Cultural Identity of Regional and Immigrant Groups." *Sociologia Ruralis* 20 (1980): 151–64.

Boissevain, Jeremy. "Family and Kinship Among the Italians in Montreal." In *The Canadian Family*, edited by K. Ishwaran, pp. 506–17. Toronto, 1976.

Campisi, P. J. "The Italian Family in the United States." *American Journal of Sociology* 53 (1948): 443–48.

Firth, Raymond. "Kinship Organization of Italianates in London." In *Two Studies of Kinship in London*, edited by R.E. Firth, pp. 67–94. London, 1956.

Lopreato, Joseph. *Peasants No More*. San Francisco, 1967.

Van Gennep, Arnold. *The Rites of Passage*. 1909. Reprint, Chicago, 1960.

Vecoli, Rudolph J. "Cult and Occult in Italian-American Culture: The Persistence of a Religious Heritage." In *Immigrants and Religion in Urban America*, edited by R.M. Miller and T.D. Marzik, pp. 25–48. Philadelphia, 1977.

White, Leslie A. *The Evolution of Culture*. New York, 1959.

Williams, Phyllis P. *Southern Italian Folkways in Europe and in America*. New Haven, Conn., 1938.

Tradition and Transition in a California Paese*

Paola A. Sensi-Isolani

Sonoma County, roughly sixty miles north of San Francisco and the wine making center of California, has attracted Italians since the late 1860s. Occidental, a village of approximately 1,750 people, is located in a valley ten miles east of the coast and ten miles west of Santa Rosa, the county seat. Outsiders who come to Occidental's Italian restaurants see the village as Italian. They notice the old Italian waitresses, the family pictures on the walls, the *bocce* court, and the Italian Hall, and are struck by all the Italian names. But in reality Occidental is no longer an Italian *paese*, and the older Italians are well aware of it.

Because Occidental Italians have been relatively isolated from prevailing attitudes and prejudices, their migration experience has in some ways been unique. By settling in a remote California *paese*, they avoided the difficult transition that many of their compatriots were forced to make as they left their villages and settled in large industrial centers in the United States. Until World War II these immigrants managed to recreate their own Italian village in Occidental, and their isolation made it easier for them to preserve their language and culture. This paper traces the history of the Italian settlement in Occidental and the village's cultural transition in recent times.

* Prof. Sensi-Isolani's presentation at the conference was made possible through a St. Mary's College Faculty Development Grant.

In 1870 there were 1,407 people in the area known as Bodega Township, which included Occidental and four other villages. Most of these people lived on ranches scattered in the nearby hills and valleys and some of them, though not Italian citizens, were Swiss Italians who had come to the United States in the early 1860s from Canton Ticino.[1] In 1877 a narrow-gauge railway was completed from Sausalito (across the bay from San Francisco) to Duncan's Mill, near Occidental. When the trains began to run regularly Occidental grew rapidly as a shipping point for fruits from farms to the east and milk and cheese from local dairies. By April 1877 three large lumber mills also were operating nearby.[2]

A few Italians began arriving in the Occidental area with the advent of the railroad. In 1880, three years after the railroad was completed, there were only thirteen Italians in the Bodega-Occidental area, none of them in the village of Occidental. All of the early Italians were from Lombardy (which borders on Canton Ticino) and were unmarried men who worked at the Swiss Italian dairies. Most were illiterate and in the *Census Field Notes* were classed as unskilled workers.

The years from 1880 to 1920, which saw the heaviest flow of Italian immigrants to California, coincided with a significant increase in the Italian population of the Occidental area. Most Italian immigrants to Occidental came from Lombardy and Tuscany. The *Lombardi* were the first to come to the area, employed first in the dairies of the Swiss Italians and then in the lumber mills north of Occidental. The *Toscani* followed shortly after, few working in the dairies, most finding employment in the lumber industry.

There were several forces at work that pushed newly arrived immigrants out of San Francisco and into the surrounding countryside. One

---

[1] Before 1900 statistical information for Occidental is merged with four other villages which made up Bodega Township. Information for each village in the township is available only from the *Census Field Notes*, on microfilm in the National Archives. Specific statistical information on Occidental is not available after 1900. To estimate the Italian-born and second- and third-generation Italian population in the village I have used the following sources: baptismal records and voter registration lists; secondary sources; and information from Italians now living in Occidental. To determine the total population of Occidental, difficult because the village is unincorporated and therefore has no boundaries, I have used the following information: post office mailboxes and home deliveries; secondary sources; and information from the Sonoma County Economic Development Board and the State of California Highway Department.

[2] M.E. Trussel, "Settlement of the Bodega Bay Region" (M.A. thesis, University of California, Berkeley, 1960), p. 28.

of these was the network nature of migration. Italians from Canton Ticino already in the area recruited neighboring *Lombardi*, relatives and acquaintances who were familiar with dairying. Beyond this pull of migration networks, however, was the fact that immigrants who arrived in San Francisco were encouraged by the Italian colony there to settle outside of the city in the agricultural interior of the state. There was a feeling on the part of both the San Francisco Italian colony and the Italian emigration authorities that encouraging Italians to seek employment outside San Francisco would avoid conflicts with established unions in the city.[3]

Italian immigration to Sonoma County was also encouraged because strong anti-Chinese sentiment had driven Chinese workers out of the county. As a result, there was a need for labor both in the lumber industry, where the Chinese worked as lumbermen and cooks, and in agriculture, where prior to 1880 the Chinese had formed the bulk of the labor force.[4]

The Italians who settled in the Occidental area in the 1880s were, for the most part, single men who worked in the dense redwood forests. Although it was reported that there were "timber mills located on most every canyon in the county where there were trees worth cutting," most of these mills were small and hired only a few hands who lived in shacks scattered around the countryside. Italians worked in these mills, peeling the tanbark which was shipped to nearby tanneries. In addition, because the immigrants from Lucca were expert *carbonari*, or charcoal makers, they acquired a virtual monopoly on the charcoal production in the Occidental area. By the end of the 1880s Occidental had become the main shipping point for western Sonoma County, and most of the lumber products shipped (in 1888 14,000 sacks of charcoal and 1,336 cords of tanbark, as well as cordwood, posts, pickets, and shingles) bore the imprint of Italian labor.[5]

By 1900, when the population of the village of Occidental numbered no more than 150, there were 156 Italians in the vicinity. A

---

[3] Deanna Gumina, *The Italians of San Francisco 1850–1930* (New York, 1978), pp. 3, 133.

[4] Ernest Ingersoll, "In a Redwood Logging Camp," *Harper's Monthly Magazine,* January 1883, pp. 193–210.

[5] Patricia Bauer, "The History of Lumbering and Tanning in Sonoma County, California, Since 1812" (M.A. thesis, University of California, Berkeley, 1958), p. 104.

few had managed to buy some land, or had opened boardinghouses and hotels in the village, but most of them were laborers, burners, or wood choppers.[6] Although they are listed in the census as holding one job, it would be misleading to assume that they followed only a single occupation throughout the year. Since much of the work was seasonal, they diversified their skills as much as possible to make up a particular *combinazione*, or viable combination of jobs. Thus, one immigrant could in the course of a year work as a lumberman, burn charcoal, peel tanbark, and hire himself out to clear someone's land, while at the same time he could run his own ranch.[7]

The Italians living in Occidental at this time can be divided into two categories: those who had been in the United States—but not necessarily in the Occidental area—since the 1870s; and those who had arrived in the late 1880s and 1890s. The first group, which consisted of six men, five of them married and with children, all owned land by 1900. The second group was composed of more recent immigrants, many of whom were relatives of the first arrivals.

During the next two decades the Italian population of Occidental increased.[8] Much of the redwood had by this time been logged out, but employment in lumber-related activities was still available. Until the late 1920s charcoal production was a very important industry in the area:

> Among the many industries, charcoal is certainly one of the most important. From the immense forested areas of the surrounding countryside, tons and tons of wood are brought to the city each month to be turned into charcoal .... The emigrants, the Italians, have made a

---

[6] U.S. Department of the Interior, Census Office, *Twelfth Census of the United States, 1900: Field Notes, State of California, Sonoma County* (microfilm, National Archives, Washington, D.C.).

[7] This occupational pattern, where the cultivator "combines a variety of different means of sustenance—from different pieces of land owned, rented, sharecropped, from wage labor, sporadic nonagricultural pursuits and anything else he can improvise," is still typical of Italian peasants. Sydel F. Silverman, "The Italian Land Reform: Some Problems in the Development of a Cultural Tradition," *Anthropological Quarterly*, April 1971, pp. 66–77.

[8] By 1930 the following Italian families lived in Occidental (with their children, they numbered 353): Gonnella, Donati, Guidici, Montafi, Taddeucci, Frati, Rossi, Binachi, Giovannini, Alberigi, Franceschi, Mazzotti, Fiori, Rossini, Boldrini, Pelletti, Coli, Panelli, Del Chiaro, Lunardi, Paladini, Brambani, Morenzoni, Gobbetti, Calvi, Panizzera, Faccendini, Morelli, Brusa, Chiaroni, Pieroni, Pozzi, Marra, Pensabene, Mazza, Cataneo, Gabrielli, Alessandrini, Traversi, Vaccarezza, Travalini, Norsia, Tenuta.

monopoly even of this charcoal industry, and have wanted to absorb the various markets.[9]

Since the first charcoal burners were from the mountain villages in the province of Lucca, Italian immigrants who followed later also tended to come from that area.

At this point many Italians, instead of working for larger operators, were self-employed. They began to contract to clear land for orchards, vineyards, or grazing, and from the stumpage and other materials they cleared they made charcoal or cut the hardwood into logs. Because the logging industry was notorious for waste, discarding smaller trees and leaving ten-foot redwood stumps, Italians opened small lumber mills where they made use of this wood, cutting it into pickets, fence posts, and shingles. Besides charcoal and redwood, tanbark was still in demand and tan oaks were cut down both for the bark and for the wood, which "was in great demand in San Francisco by the U.S. Mint and bakers, since it burns up completely and with little smoke."[10] One Italian family, taking advantage of the local residents' desire to clear the area of trees and brush, developed a business selling Christmas trees and making wreaths from redwood brush. Italian immigrants capitalized on their ingenuity and their ability to make profitable what others considered useless.

Italians also found work in agriculture. As more land was cleared, fruit and berry orchards were planted and hops were cultivated. During the picking season these ventures employed thousands.[11] Although most wineries in Sonoma County were located to the northeast in the Napa Valley, Occidental had three wineries by 1919. One of these was owned by Italians, and all of them depended on Italian expertise and labor. Because of the railroad, Occidental was also a convenient stop for travelers coming from San Francisco to the Russian River and nearby Camp Meeker. Each summer the farms, dairies, and orchards of the Occidental area fed these vacationers. Many of the people who came from San Francisco by train on day trips stopped to eat in Occidental, which by 1900 had become famous for its Italian restaurants.

---

[9] G.M. Tuoni and G. Brogelli, *Attività italiane in California* (San Francisco, 1924), p. 249. Translation mine.

[10] Bauer, "Lumbering and Tanning," p. 33; Ingersoll, "Redwood Logging Camp," p. 199.

[11] Healdsburg Chamber of Commerce, *Healdsburg, Sonoma County* (San Francisco, 1909), p. 14.

For many Italians, outside employment did not mean relinquishing the land they had bought, nor did it decrease their interest in buying land. In fact, because of the decreasing profitability of the logging industry, land could be bought relatively cheaply. By owning land and knowing how to make a living on it, those Italians who lost their winery jobs during Prohibition were able to survive. Many Italians also struggled through the Depression by living off their ranches and working at odd jobs.

Although there does not seem to have been animosity between them, the immigrants from Lombardy and Tuscany were culturally different.[12] The *Lombardi* came for the most part from the province of Sondrio in the area between Lago di Como and the Swiss border. They were peasants who eked out an existence raising a few cows, cultivating their small plots, and chopping wood. The great majority had little in the way of education; many could not read or write, spoke only in dialect and had but a cursory knowledge of standard Italian. The *Toscani* came from the province of Lucca, most from the mountain villages of Coreglia Antelminelli and nearby Barga. Some were *mezzadri*, sharecroppers who cultivated the landlord's holding for a percentage of the crop. Most, however, were small landowners who supplemented their family's income by working as *figurinai*, traveling throughout the world manufacturing and selling plaster figurines. Unlike the *Lombardi*, most *Toscani*, both men and women, were literate, and their Italian was considered far superior to the Lombard dialect. One *Lombardo* who arrived in 1922 told me that he learned to speak real Italian only after he came to Occidental; it was the *Toscani* who taught him real Italian, he said.

In Italy the *Toscani* were not as isolated from the urban centers and their "civilizing" values as were the *Lombardi*. The peasants of Coreglia and Barga had been traveling abroad as *figurinai* since the sixteenth century. Visits to the nearby towns of Lucca, Bagni di Lucca, and Pistoia were common, and both Coreglia and Barga had been resort areas for centuries, attracting the gentry of such towns

---

[12] The information in the following sections was obtained in 26 interviews conducted from July to October 1981 with members of the immigrant, second, third, and fourth generations, as well as non-Italians. In-depth interviews were conducted with the following people: Giuseppe and Giuseppina Faccendini, Adeline and Samuele Chiaroni, and Elizabeth Mazzotti. To them I would like to express my deepest gratitude. Many of the interviews were conducted in Italian; my English translations appear in this article.

as Prato and Florence. Their exposure to the outside world and its values was much greater than that of the *Lombardi*, most of whom lived in remote mountain villages. One of my Lombard informants pointed out that until he went into the army in 1918 he knew nothing of the world; the only time he left his village was in the summer months, when he brought the cows to their mountain pasture. To the *Lombardi*, therefore, the *Toscani* seemed sophisticated. A Lombard woman who came to the Occidental area with her family in 1907 told me that "we poor *Lombardi* looked like such country bumpkins compared to those *Toscani*."

Although Italians in general were attracted to the area by the lumber industry, individual Italians came because of social and kinship networks. Because of these networks, most Occidental Italians originated from only a few Tuscan and Lombard villages. This regional homogeneity was further encouraged by the employment agencies of San Francisco, which often directed new arrivals to jobs in outlying areas. These Italian labor agents, well aware that regional identity was much more important to the immigrants than national identity, were careful to send employers men from the same region of Italy.[13]

The network nature of this migration and the role of employment agencies can be seen in the story of the brother of one of my informants, who came to San Francisco in 1904 from a mountain village in Lombardy:

> The emigrants would stop [in San Francisco]. There were agencies who looked for work for these emigrants. These Morellis had bought a bit of land near here. Now they were looking for Italians to work the land and they got in touch with these agencies. My brother was sent out by an agency to work for these Morellis. The Morellis were *Lombardi* like us, we spoke the same dialect.

This brother worked for his Italian employers for two years, until the employment agency told him he could earn five to six dollars a day in the coal mines of Wyoming. While in Wyoming he sent for two of his brothers from Italy. After six years he returned to Occidental with one brother and bought land near the Morelli ranch. Two more brothers arrived from Italy, and by 1922 there were four brothers in Occidental. The youngest brother recalled for me his early experiences:

---

[13] "Italians as Farmers and Fruit Growers," *Outlook*, September 1908, pp. 87–88.

I worked in the ranches, they all belonged to Italians then. If you wanted to milk cows you could find work everywhere. It was always the first job for us *Lombardi*. I would work for one a few years and then go to another. Savings? I worked for an Albini and I spent twenty-four dollars in 19 months. I earned sixty dollars a month and they furnished food and we slept in a cabin .... In '28 I bought this land and paid back my brother for the price of the ticket.

Eventually one brother returned to Italy; the other two went home to marry but returned to Occidental.

Regional and family networks also brought the *Toscani* to Occidental. Ermenegildo Gonnella, who emigrated from Coreglia in 1894, was responsible for the arrival of twenty-eight family members by 1907. (In Occidental the name Gonnella is said to be equivalent to Smith.)

Except for better economic opportunities and the possibility of buying land, the life of the Occidental Italians was not very different from their life in Italy. Once Italians owned land they strived for self-sufficiency. They raised cows, pigs, and chickens, planted fruit orchards, a vegetable garden, and a small vineyard, and lived primarily on what they raised and hunted. Men made money through a combination of ranching, free enterprise in the lumber business, and occasional wage labor.

Women washed and cooked, baked bread in beehive-shaped ovens built near the house, made butter and *ricotta* to sell, took care of the chickens, and picked berries:

> We did everything at the ranch. With the pig we made sausages, *biroldo*, ham, and pigskin which we ate with beans. We had chickens. My mother made cheese and *ricotta* with the milk of our cows .... We used to pick fruit and we picked berries at 3 in the morning, then we sold them.

Families of first-generation Italians, in particular those who lived on ranches, were large. At certain times of the year the entire family would go and pick hops in the surrounding hopyards. In 1909, local chamber of commerce pamphlets described field work in glowing terms:

> The large fields give employment to thousands of hands during the picking season. These pickers generally camp out on ground furnished free by their employer. Good pickers make from $3-5 per day, besides enjoying the relaxation and charm of camp life.[14]

---

[14] Healdsburg Chamber of Commerce, *Healdsburg*, p. 19.

In contrast, the son of Italian immigrants who used to pick hops with his family remembered conditions differently:

We went to the hopyards and picked hops. Slept in tents, we used to live like tramps, like Mexicans. Every year we went hop picking, women and children went. We stayed two weeks. I often think of that. What a life. Five kids, whole families in tents like dogs. It was hard in that hopyard. I want to show you a picture of us working in the hopyards. Just like Mexicans.

Italians who worked for the railroad, owned shops, or ran saloons and hotels, lived in the village of Occidental. They were more committed to the wage economy; their work pattern was not as diverse as that of the Italians who lived on the land, nor were they as self-sufficient. Women in this group also worked. They cooked, cleaned, and served in the hotels, kept boarders, took in washing, and worked in shops.

Although much has been said about the gregariousness of Italians and their preference for life in villages or towns, the Italians of Occidental did not look upon life on the ranch as undesirable. This could be because few people lived in isolation (as many of the Swiss Italians did); relatives and neighbors were close, and socializing between families and friends was easy and frequent.

Social activities took many forms. In the earlier days, while there were many more men than women in the area, saloons and dance halls were the primary attraction. But their importance was challenged by fraternal orders. By 1898 there were six lodges in Occidental; one of them, the 94th Grove of the United Ancient Order of Druids (founded in 1893 by Giuseppe Morelli), was made up entirely of Italians and Swiss Italians.[15]

A 1916 survey conducted by the Presbyterian church reported that "the social life of the foreign element, particularly in communities where they predominate, very largely centers about their lodges."[16] There is no doubt that an important function of the Druids was socializing. The Druid meeting hall was a place where Italian men could gather and where newly arrived immigrants from Italy were made to feel at home and could receive advice from older and more experienced

---

[15] *Illustrated Atlas of Sonoma County* (Santa Rosa, 1898), p. 52.

[16] California Board of Home Missions of the Presbyterian Church, Department of Church and Country Life, *A Rural Survey of Marin and Sonoma Counties* (New York, 1916), p. 52.

Picking hops near Occidental, 1918. Photo courtesy of Sam Chiaroni.

immigrants. Because the Druids separated the sexes into a male organization and a female circle (founded in 1914), they provided the type of all-male socializing that was most familiar to Italians who came from small villages. For these Italian male immigrants, the Occidental Druid meetings were equivalent to the Italian village cafes, where men gathered to argue, drink, and play cards.

The Druids forbade discussion of politics and religion at meetings, yet they did instill a moral code in their members. "They have a prayer that just about says it better than any in the Catholic church," said one of my informants, who has been a member of the Druid Women's Circle since 1936. "They believe in a hereafter, in the soul. Druids are religious. We ask God for guidance and blessing and strength and courage to get us through the day. They're upright."

Members of the Druids paid dues, which went into a fund that entitled members to certain benefits if disabled and that compensated widows. As in most fraternal organizations, the Druids were encouraged to help each other in difficult times. The Druids, who owned the Occidental cemetery, accompanied the coffin in funeral processions.

The Druids also were seen by their Italian founders in Occidental as a force to counter the influence of the Catholic church. For this reason the more religious Italian families in Occidental were opposed to the group. Many of these Italians refused to be buried in the Druid cemetery, insisting that they be taken to the Catholic cemetery in Bodega, approximately ten miles away.

The Italian community in Occidental was close-knit; most socializing was done with other Italians. A woman born in the village in 1909 remembers her youth:

> We sang in chorus, some alto, others bass. We went to the house of friends or relatives, we danced. Someone had a guitar, someone a harmonica. We played *morra* and cards, but my brothers mainly played *morra*. We drank.

As long as the railway ran through the village, Occidental was the center of a great deal of social activity. When Italians from the surrounding area went into the village to buy supplies, they would stop for a drink or to discuss the latest news. In addition to hotels and shops, in the 1920s and 1930s Occidental had three pool halls, several saloons, and *bocce* courts. Suppers, picnics, barbecues and dances were organized; the most important event of the year was on the Fourth of July, when Italian bands were brought to the village and people came from miles around to celebrate.

The Catholic church in Occidental was built in 1903; most of the money and labor were donated by Italians. Unlike the church in most villages in Italy, however, the Occidental church did not play a central role in the life of the Italian community. The Italians of Occidental differed in their attitudes toward Catholicism. In general, the *Lombardi* were less religious than the *Toscani*. There were, of course, exceptions, but it is no coincidence that the *Lombardi* were instrumental in founding the Druid lodge, while many more *Toscani* than *Lombardi* were involved in the construction of the church.

Although some families were very devout, I was told that in general Occidental Italians were not religious. This is corroborated by the 1916 Presbyterian church survey:

> The Italians and Swiss Italians are nominally Catholic. A very considerable number of these have practically or entirely broken the hold which the Catholic church has had upon them and although they could not by any stretch of the imagination be considered Protestant, they are Catholic only in the most formal and external fashion, if at all.

The survey goes on to say that "many Italians in the area have identified themselves with a form of socialistic propaganda that is definitely anti-Christian."[17] It is difficult to discover just what the political ideas of first-generation immigrants were. During interviews none of the three first-generation immigrants remembered any political involvement on the part of Italians. Socialist ideas were discussed in the lumber camps, because, as one of my respondents pointed out, "in the camps, the workers were dominated by the masters, they were subjugated. To detach themselves from capitalism they spoke of socialism or of communism." But most of these lumber camps were small; immigrants lived in cabins with one or two other people and sometimes with wives and children, not in large groups. There is no evidence of strikes or labor activity in the area as there was farther north in California among Italians in the large lumber camps.[18]

If Italians had political ideas, they were hesitant to talk about them. I was told that "in the old days, in order to avoid discord, people hesitated to talk about politics." When the lumbering days were over, those Italians who remained in the area owned their land or

---

[17] Ibid., pp. 9–10.
[18] James T. Hudson, "The McCloud River Affair of 1909: A Study in the Use of State Troops," *California Historical Society Quarterly* 25 (March 1956): 30–31.

had their own small family businesses. Consequently, the individuality often identified with capitalism appealed to them: "*A me però, piace lavorare da solo, essere libero*" (I like to work by myself, to be free). This desire expressed to me by one immigrant was shared by most Italians in the area.

Within the Italian community, and of course within the family, immigrants and their children spoke Italian. Among the *Lombardi*, however, dialect was spoken within the family and with fellow *Lombardi*, whereas standard Italian was spoken among the *Toscani* and between the two groups. The children of these immigrants, many born between 1900 and 1920, still speak excellent Italian. Among the *Toscani* in particular, there seems to have been pride in the language and a determination to maintain it and teach it to one's children. One informant born in Occidental in 1910 remembers that when she and her sister returned from school, her father (a shoemaker and shopkeeper who had immigrated with his family to Occidental in 1888 when he was eleven years old) gave them lessons in Italian. The oral tradition in the village also was very strong, especially among *Toscani*. Older Italians remember *fole* (fairy tales) and the *stornelli* their mothers sang as they worked.

Because of its cultural and geographic isolation, until the late 1920s the Occidental Italian community was endogamous; with few exceptions Italians married Italians. This was true of immigrants who came to Occidental from Italy as young men and women and also of most of the second generation born in the village of Italian parents. Until the 1920s men outnumbered women and were often related to them. As a result, first-cousin marriage was common and the marriage of distant cousins even more common. In one family, there were four first-cousin marriages in the first generation.[19]

There is no doubt that northern European settlers looked down on the Italians. The *Petaluma Argus*, for example, refers to them as "the Italians" where for other groups they would use the family name: "Notice of delinquent taxes 1878-79. Harrison, George, 160 acres, bounded on the north by Stites, east by Irwin, south by Bones, west by Italians." Prejudice was often quite open, as can be seen in this letter written to the *Argus* in June 1887: "I hear that they're

---

[19] In a pattern that is typical of villages in Italy, the same Italian surnames are common in Occidental, and relationships are difficult to unravel because everyone is related to everyone else.

going to build a new dance hall for Italians. My, what a smelly place that's going to be!"[20]

Although Italians began coming to the Occidental area in large numbers in the 1890s, attitudes toward them had not changed substantially two decades later. The Presbyterian *Rural Survey* points out that in 1916 Italian groups in rural Sonoma County lived in virtual segregation:

> As a result some of the smaller towns are not very markedly American in characteristic . . . . [These Italians demonstrate] a very high degree of thrift and industry, but a very low degree of general intelligence and education. [There is a] great lack of literary and cultural opportunities in the homes and the community, a dominant part played socially by foreign (Italian) lodges and by the saloons, and a general sentiment opposed to secondary and higher education and to other influences which would probably result in the more thorough Americanization of the community.[21]

In spite of prejudice and cultural isolation, by the late 1920s some Occidental Italians had begun to succeed in business, and histories of Sonoma County, which always include biographies of prominent citizens, include them. Some of these Italians became Masons, which is an indication both of their success, since in the Occidental area only the most affluent could belong, and of their Americanization, since membership in Masonic lodges had in the past been forbidden to Catholics and Italians.

The Occidental Italian community was affected by world events and Italy's involvement in them. At the beginning most supported Fascism. *Faccetta Nera* was a popular song in the village, villagers had pictures of Mussolini in their homes, and some sent their gold wedding rings home to support Mussolini. But by the time the United States had entered the war, most Italians were resigned to the fact that they had sons fighting on the American side, and nephews and other close relatives on the Italian side. During World War II, most of the sons of Occidental Italians fought in Europe, and many of them were involved in the Allied landing at Anzio. A few met relatives in Italy, and after the war six Italian relatives of Occidental Italians

---

[20] *Petaluma Argus*, 3 January 1879, p. 2; 12 June 1887, p. 3.

[21] California Board of Home Missions of the Presbyterian Church, *Rural Survey*, pp. 19–20.

immigrated. They were the last of a migration that had begun almost a hundred years before.

Until the Second World War the Occidental Italians lived in a community that was to a large extent both culturally and geographically closed. Of the roughly 500 people who lived in the area, close to 400 were Italians or of Italian descent, and Occidental was regarded by outsiders as a village of Italians.

In the late 1930s train service from San Francisco to Duncan's Mill was discontinued. This marked the end of an era for Occidental, since its economic existence depended to a large extent on the railway, which kept it in close contact with San Francisco's vacationers and markets. Without the train, Occidental became more isolated, and with fewer business and employment opportunities the population decreased. After the railway was removed, Occidental's primary attraction was the Italian food served at the village's three hotels. These hotels provided work for many Italians in the community, most of them relatives and friends of the owners.

In the 1940s the population of Occidental decreased; many of those who left were Italians. Reasons for departure were partly economic and partly the result of acculturation. Many who left were second-generation Italians married to non-Italians.

During the past twenty years Occidental has seen a different kind of immigration. In the 1960s disaffected young people from cities flocked to the area. As a result of this migration there are now three communes near the village. In the 1970s urbanites, many of them professionals who could afford skyrocketing land prices, moved to the village.[22]

> Most of the Italians have gone, you know, moved to greener pastures, or they have passed on. Who's left? The Guidicis, there were two sons. Who's left? Only one is here with his wife. The Montafis, there is only one son here with his wife. The Guidicis have the Calvi girl. Who's left? Two of the Guidicis out of thirteen children, and of course the Giovanninis; there's none left of the Giovanninis at all. Of Dionisio's family there's only Viola Beedle in Occidental, and that was a large family. How about the Donatis? Nisio was the last of those. Old Man

---

[22] The increase in the population in the village and surrounding area between 1960 and 1980 is reflected in the number of post boxes and rural deliveries in 1964 and 1981:
1964—232 P.O. boxes, 190 rural deliveries.
1981—600 P.O. boxes, 300 rural deliveries.

Negri has gone, the Pelettis have moved on, the Fioris are in Santa Rosa.

The above statement, made to me by an Italian American woman born in 1903, indicates the reasons for the decline of the Italian population in Occidental. Most of the older native Italians have died, and the younger second- and third-generation Italian Americans have moved out of the area in search of work.

There are now fifteen Italian American families with roughly seventy members left in Occidental. Since the village population is estimated at 1,750, residents of Italian extraction are obviously now very much in the minority. Yet, because of their long presence in the village and the nature of the businesses they run (the Italian restaurants), Occidental is still considered an Italian town by outsiders. Indeed, looking at the names of the businesses—Gonnella, Panizzera, Negri, Fiori, Calvi, Lunardi, Matteri—one would think that only Italians lived here. The volunteer fire department is made up largely of Italian Americans, and the village is administered by a committee of three, Louis Gonnella, Dan Gonnella, and Elizabeth Mazzotti, all cousins.

As a result of the new migration, however, the village is divided into two camps: the native residents, many of them Italian Americans, who have lived and worked in the village for most of their life; and the new residents, many of whom are professionals who work in the cities or the unemployed who live on welfare. The newcomers, referred to as *Americani* by the Italian American residents, now dominate the school board; they run many of the smaller tourist-oriented shops and claim that the villagers have little concern for civic and environmental issues. Because of their numerical strength and political activism, they are beginning to influence policies that affect the village.

The Italians who live in the village see themselves as the children and grandchildren of the pioneers who made the village what it is. There is no doubt that the Italian immigrants were responsible for the way the village and surrounding countryside now look. The features of Occidental that tourists and newcomers find so attractive, the Catholic church, the older village houses, the countryside with its fields, fruit orchards, and small vineyards, are primarily the result of the hard work of the Italian immigrants who settled in Occidental and its vicinity.

The Italian Americans over thirty-five years of age, who are the children and grandchildren of the original immigrants, say that their parents and grandparents were fiercely proud of their Italian heritage. It is because of this, they say, that they were taught to speak Italian. It is quite common for third-generation Italian Americans who have never set foot in Italy to speak excellent Italian. Only in a few homes, however, is Italian now spoken spontaneously instead of English. None of the Occidental Italian Americans under twenty-five, even the children of Italian-born immigrants, can speak Italian, although many of them do understand it and can manage a few expressions, most of them exclamations or profanities.

The fact that younger Italian Americans do not speak Italian is one result of the changes that have opened Occidental to the outside world. By the end of the Second World War communication with surrounding cities was easier, economic opportunities in cities had increased, and television was becoming an important entertainment medium.

Occidental's loss of its relative isolation after the war is reflected in the rapid acculturation of the newer Italian immigrants. The speed with which a Lombard woman, who emigrated to Occidental in 1946, learned English and found work outside the community contrasts sharply with the experiences of the earlier Italian immigrants who barely learned English, spoke Italian with their children, and worked within a few miles of the village.[23] The woman told me that when she arrived in 1946 she was determined to learn English. She learned to drive, got a job ten miles away as a dishwasher in a school cafeteria, and by 1964 had worked her way to cafeteria manager. Although she and her husband speak the Lombard dialect and Italian, they usually speak English at home because, as she says, "I forced him to speak English to me so that I'd learn." Of their three sons, born in 1948, '49, and '52, only the eldest speaks some Italian and has an Italian name. "For the others we said, why give them Italian names if they stay in America?"

Another difference between the old and new immigrants is in the time lag between arrival in the United States and naturalization. The Lombard woman's husband, who came to Occidental from Lombardy in 1922 when he was twenty-two years old, did not apply for natural-

---

[23] With the exception of one older woman, the six Italians (one Lombard and five Tuscans) who immigrated to Occidental after 1945 assimilated much more quickly than did their relatives who had come earlier.

ization until he was over forty and had been in the United States for twenty years. This time lag between arrival and citizenship is common in the older immigrant group in Occidental. Reasons expressed include a poor knowledge of English and a long-held intention to return to Italy. In contrast, the Lombard woman who arrived in 1946 at the age of twenty-six rushed to get citizenship, waiting only the minimum time required.

The second- and third-generation Italian Americans, who themselves speak Italian, and whose children do not, expressed concern that their children were not taught Italian in school while Spanish, German, and French were offered. However, these parents have made no effort to pressure the school district to teach Italian. They are aware that their children are losing their Italian culture but they seem resigned to the idea. One parent remarked, "You get mixed up here and pretty quick just your name is Italian and that's it. I don't like it, myself. There isn't a hell of a lot I can do about it, though."[24]

The young Occidental Italian Americans, most of whom are third- and fourth-generation descendants of the original immigrants, are aware of their Italian identity. Most expressed a desire to visit Italy and regret that their parents had not taught them Italian. There does, however, seem to be a gulf between the younger and the older generations. The older Italian Americans are afraid of the values of young people, particularly what they define as free love and drugs. They also feel that the young people do not understand hard work, that their life has been too easy, and that as a result they are spoiled. "If you tell younger people today what life used to be like, they won't believe you," said a 77-year-old daughter of Tuscan immigrants. "Young people today have changed; now you see things that when I was young would have made our hair stand on end." Except for family get-togethers, activities are segregated by age. The Druid lodge, for example, which still is composed primarily of Italian Americans,

---

[24] They may be realistic in feeling that they can do nothing about this. Speaking to a second-generation Italian American from the nearby city of Santa Rosa, I learned that the large Italian community there had put pressure on both the junior college and the high school districts to teach Italian. There is now a night class offered by the junior college, but the district has no intention of offering Italian in the high school, where the Italian American community feels it is much more important. The general attitude of school officials, as reported to me by some Italian American residents of Santa Rosa, seems to be that unlike French, German, and Spanish, Italian has little in the way of cultural value and would attract only students of Italian descent.

has no young people in either its men's lodge or women's circle.

In spite of tensions between young and old, ties are still very strong within the family. Occidental Italians prefer to work with their families. The eight family businesses in the village all are run by Italians who primarily hire Italian relatives and friends. Residence patterns also reflect those close ties; adult children or grandchildren often live with their parents or in an adjoining house.

These close family ties, along with a general suspicion of education, which for most Occidental Italians has meant the outside world and its values, have kept many Italian Americans from encouraging their children to go to college. For the earlier immigrants a college education was virtually impossible. Parents lacked money and their children did not attend school beyond the eighth grade because there was no high school nearby. But this is not the case for the grandchildren and great-grandchildren who have gone to high school and whose parents are financially secure. The desire emphasized during my interviews was for one's son to work in the family business. This has in fact been the option for many Italian American young people, particularly for the boys.[25] If there is no family business, sons are encouraged to learn a trade rather than go to college. Even when Occidental Italians move away from the area and send their children to college, aspirations are not high, and the occupational preference seems to be high school teacher or probation officer rather than doctor or lawyer.

Lack of a college education doesn't mean that these Italian Americans are not affluent. Those who own businesses, especially the two family restaurants, have done very well. One restaurant owner, for example, owns a string of racehorses. Although not all the Italian families who own businesses are so obviously well off, they are comfortable. Many of the older Italian Americans live on Social Security (sometimes supplemented with income from odd jobs), and sometimes on money they have earned from selling pieces of land to the new arrivals.

Until very recently many Italians were employed for the two months before Christmas making wreaths and garlands of redwood brush. This business, which was begun in 1897 by two brothers who moved to Occidental from Coreglia in Tuscany, is still run by the same family

---

[25] Although immigrant Italian women always worked, there doesn't seem to be as much concern that young women work today. Young women still are expected to marry and spend most of their time raising children.

and generates more than $200,000 yearly in sales. At present there are only two Italian American women, both relatives of the owner, still making these wreaths. "Most of the Italians," remarked Ben Gonnella, who owns the business, "have moved up in the world. Used to be that all Italians in town worked on those wreaths. Now they are either too old or they have jobs and can't take the time off." Gonnella now hires Mexicans, whom he puts up in cabins at the family farm and pays on a piecework basis. Today Mexicans have replaced the Italians at low-paying seasonal jobs. Many Italians in Occidental realize that in the past their life must have resembled that of today's Mexican immigrants.

There now are few Italians who live on their own ranch; when they do, more often than not the ranch is a hobby. Although in the past families lived off what the ranch produced, the children of these Italian immigrants point out that today one cannot survive on a small ranch. They, their children, and sometimes their grandchildren are no longer satisfied with the hard work of ranch life. Their needs are greater, they say, than were the needs of their parents, and the income from ranching is limited. Those who now live on ranches have steady incomes from outside jobs. They may raise a cow for meat and have a vegetable garden, but they buy most of their supplies at the supermarket. Only two Italians make their own wine now, and only a few families make the *salame, prosciutto* and *biroldo* that all the first-generation Italians prepared.

As in the past, religion seems to be important for only a few families in the Italian community. Those families whose parents and grandparents were very religious (*fanatici*, a few of them were called by other Italian Americans I interviewed), still tend to go to church more than the others. But in general the Italians I interviewed agreed that most Italian Americans in Occidental do not go to church. In part, this can be accounted for by the growing secularization of all of society. But oddly enough, their attitude toward religion, as described to me by the village priest, is very similar to that of Italians in Italy today:

> I have been in numerous parishes up and down the coast, but none where there is as dominant an Italian community. But, surprisingly, there are only a handful who come to church. They are clannish; that may not be the right word, but somehow it seems appropriate. They seem to be more "Old Country." There, church was for the women; you hardly see any young Italian people in the church. The backbone of this community is the restaurants, but practically no restaurant

people come to church. If it's something social, oh yes .... It's not just Italians but it's characteristic of them. What alarms me is that the young people have picked up the same ways.

The village priest said that in Occidental young people go to church only for marriages and baptisms. Even then, he said, the emphasis is not on the religious part of the baptism but on the big party that is given afterward. The priest expressed the belief that the values of the older Italians would not have been passed on to the younger generation if the Italians had settled in the city:

> Not in the big cities, I'm from the big cities [Detroit and Chicago] till I came here. I never ran into this that much there. There modern Italians are different. They don't want to be associated with the old Italians that much. Here it isn't so. They want to keep that mentality. In the city, you're rubbing elbows with other people and the parish schools made a difference.

The priest's evaluation seems quite accurate to me. Unlike the Italian immigrants who settled in cities, where they found churches and parochial schools dominated by the Irish, the Occidental immigrants built their own church. They lived in relative isolation and were not pushed to deny the values of the older generation. As a result, their religious behavior still closely resembles that of native Italians.[26]

To this day Occidental retains much of its old-fashioned village character. People from nearby ranches and houses come into town to do their shopping or to pick up mail. But the vitality of the community is only a shadow of what it was, say the older residents. The supermarkets in nearby towns and the telephone have made going to the village much less necessary. The village now primarily attracts tourists who are drawn by the Italian restaurants.

The Occidental Italians, now less isolated, see changes taking place in their community. The newcomers from cities and the attitudes and values of the younger generation point toward a way of life more identified with the city than with the village. The cultural transition that their parents and grandparents avoided must now be faced. In the past, when there was a conflict between American values and their

---

[26] The priest pointed to one family as an example of modern Italians as they would be in the city: "The Rosa family—the village doctor—they're different types of Italians now, but then he's an outsider even if he's of Italian descent, and his wife is Irish. Now, he's a different type of Italian, they come to church and contribute."

own, immigrants in Occidental would draw comfort and support from the large Italian community in the village. Now, the older Italians, most of them in their sixties and seventies, know they are alone. Neither the younger generation nor the newcomers understand them. No one, they feel, appreciates the sacrifices and hard work of the Italian pioneers who made the village and surrounding countryside what it is today. It is to record the work, dedication, and tenacity with which these Italian immigrants clung to their language and culture that this article has been written.

Italian Farmers in Cumberland

John Andreozzi

The Italian immigration to North America was basically a movement from Mediterranean farming towns to cities. Much has been written about the Italians who took up urban residence and industrial jobs in America. Less known are the Italian farming communities in the United States.[1] Two of the oldest rural colonies were located in Wisconsin. The colony at Genoa dates back to 1863, when a handful of northern Italian families began farming near the Mississippi River. Twenty years later southern Italians established a large farming community 140 miles north in Cumberland.[2]

This paper will examine the Italian experience in Cumberland, where the immigrants forged their livelihood from a creative com-

---

[1] U.S. Immigration Commission, *Reports of the Immigration Commission*, vol. 21, *Immigrants in Industries: Pt. 24, Recent Immigrants in Agriculture*, 61st Cong., 2d sess., S. Doc. no. 633 (Washington, D.C., 1911), details forty-three Italian farming communities throughout the United States, each composed of from 2 to 956 households (report hereafter referred to as *Recent Immigrants in Agriculture*). Another study lists fifteen additional Italian rural communities in existence by 1910. See Luciano J. Iorizzo and Salvatore Mondello, *The Italian Americans* (New York, 1971), pp. 221–22.

[2] *Recent Immigrants in Agriculture*, pp. 390, 411–12. With approximately 250 Italian families, the Cumberland settlement tied the Independence, La., colony as the fourth largest Italian colony studied by the Immigration Commission. Vineland, N.J., was the largest settlement, numbering 956 households.

bination of farming and railroad work. Both Cumberland and Genoa were among forty-three Italian agricultural colonies investigated by the U.S. Immigration Commission early in this century. While the commission praised the northern Italians in Genoa, it held a most disparaging and bigoted view of Cumberland's *meridionali*. This paper will attempt to present a more balanced account of the Cumberland settlement and provide the Italian perspective that was so obviously omitted by government investigators in 1909.

Cumberland is located in northwestern Wisconsin, some 85 miles northeast of St. Paul, Minnesota. Lying on what was originally an island in Beaver Dam Lake, it was known as the "Island City." The first homesteaders arrived in the 1870s after hearing that the Omaha Railroad was to be extended through the area. The railroad reached Cumberland in 1878 and the island was connected to the mainland by causeways. Several accounts mention a strike during construction of the railway. The foreman for the Omaha Railroad is reported to have traveled to St. Paul and hired a group of Italians to replace the strikers. When their work was completed, some of the laborers settled south of town, where they purchased a dozen railroad shanties and converted them into homes. A different version of the arrival of the first Italians comes from the 1911 report of the U.S. Immigration Commission, which states that the first Italians arrived from Chicago in 1881, after being told about "good wages, plenty of work and cheap land" in the Cumberland-Hurley area. The 1880 U.S. census does not include any Italian surnames for Cumberland, but the Wisconsin 1885 census lists thirty-five Italians, including twenty-seven members of the extended Donatelle family. Nine of the immigrants lived south of the city where the railroad curves north into Cumberland. This area was to become the center of Italian settlement in the Island City.[3]

Cumberland at this time was a town of lumberjacks and railroad workers. During the 1880s and 1890s, according to a WPA survey, "the town was one of the toughest lumber camps in Wisconsin, a member of the notorious quartette: 'Cumberland, Hurley, Hayward and Hell.' The first three, it was said, were tougher than the fourth.

[3] Cumberland Centennial Committee, *Cumberland: Wisconsin's Island City* (Cumberland, 1974), pp. 4, 31; Newton S. Gordon, *History of Barron County, Wisconsin* (Minneapolis, 1922), pp. 1097–98; *Recent Immigrants in Agriculture*, p. 412; U.S. Manuscript Census, 1880: Barron County, Wis., State Historical Society of Wisconsin, Madison; Wisconsin Manuscript Census, 1885: Barron County, State Historical Society of Wisconsin.

In 1884 Cumberland had twenty-four saloons to serve a few hundred inhabitants; in 1886 the number of saloon licenses was restricted to five at any one time." The survey goes on to describe the efforts of the town marshal who, in the tradition of the American West, single-handedly brought law and order to Cumberland.[4] Even during its turbulent pioneer days, Cumberland had a more sober side. Italians participated in Catholic church services that were held in a store, with a congregation that included French, Germans, Poles, English and Irish. In 1884 St. Mary's Church was constructed under the guidance of Father DeParadis, an Italian priest. The Italians, the largest group in the multi-ethnic congregation, soon thereafter decided to build their own church, and in 1885 they erected a building south of Cumberland. San Antonio di Abate became the second Italian parish in Wisconsin; the first was established in Genoa twenty-one years earlier. Both St. Anthony's and St. Mary's were tended over the years by one priest who lived in Cumberland.[5]

The Italian settlement, which centered around St. Anthony's Church, grew slowly from 35 inhabitants in 1885 to 62 in 1890. In that year a study of immigrants by the Wisconsin Historical Society mentioned Italians in three other locales in Wisconsin but failed to note the small Cumberland group. After 1890 the settlement grew quickly to 289 residents in 1895 and 472 in 1900.[6]

The vast majority of Cumberland's Italians were from the small communities lying between Aquila and Campobasso in Abruzzi-Molise. Included among these towns are Ateleta, Cinquemiglia, Cantalupo, Boiano, and San Polo Matese. About a dozen families from the province of Catanzaro, Calabria, and several Sicilian families also settled in the Island City. Many *Calabresi* followed the railroad construction northward to Spooner and settled there.[7]

---

[4] Work Projects Administration, *Wisconsin: A Guide to the Badger State* (New York, 1941), pp. 408–409.

[5] Gordon, *History of Barron County*, p. 1098; Fr. Richard Hermann, "The History of Our Parishes: St. Anthony's, Cumberland," (Superior, Wis.) *Catholic Herald Citizen*, 15 January 1955, p. 6; Harry Hosper Heming, *The Catholic Church in Wisconsin* (Milwaukee, 1897), p. 858.

[6] Wisconsin Manuscript Census, 1885, 1895; U.S. Manuscript Census, 1900; State Historical Society of Wisconsin, *Proceedings of the Thirty-seventh Annual Meeting* (Madison, 1890), p. 61.

[7] Tom and Ann Ricci, interview with author, Cumberland, 27 August 1981; Mary Schullo, interview with author, Cumberland, 27 August 1981; Mike and Rose Ranallo, interview with author, Cumberland, 28 August 1981; Sharon A.

A number of immigrants from San Polo Matese had been organ grinders in other American cities, a trade they learned in this country. They settled some distance from the original colony, in an elevated area southwest of the city that later became part of the township of Crystal Lake. The former organ grinders brought the tools of their trade—organ boxes, bagpipes, clarinets, and monkeys—with them to Crystal Lake, and the colony became known among local Italians as the "Monkey Settlement."[8]

Cumberland was the second or third area of settlement for most of the Italian immigrants. Many had first lived in New Orleans, Boston, New York, Baltimore, Pittsburgh, Chicago, Duluth, or St. Paul before traveling to the Island City. One immigrant, Ambrose DeGidio, left San Polo Matese in 1862 and worked on the railroads in the Boston area for twenty-eight years, while making frequent return trips to see his family in Italy. In 1890 he brought his wife and two of their children to settle in Cumberland. Gennaro Cotone and his son Felice left Cantalupo in 1882 and did railroad work in Baltimore. In 1893 Gennaro and Felice and his bride joined other relatives in Chicago. But the family grew weary of running a saloon in the tough neighborhood on Clark Street and moved to Cumberland in 1900 so they could raise their children in the country.[9]

It appears that most Italians settled in Cumberland after hearing about the availability of jobs and land through *paesani* or fellow workers. Pasquale Di Re, born in Abruzzi, was an important labor contractor in St. Paul who hired Italians for railroad construction work throughout the Upper Midwest and as far away as the West Coast. It was probably Di Re who told Sam Palmer (Savino Palmiere) and Sabatino Donatelle about opportunities in Cumberland. These men, two of the original settlers, encouraged many of their relatives and townsmen living in other parts of the United States and in Italy to

---

Tarr, *Spooner, Wisconsin: The First 100 Years* (Spooner, 1979), vol. 1, p. 16; Cumberland Centennial Committee, *Cumberland*, p. 33.

[8] Ambrose DeGidio, interview with author, Cumberland, 1 September 1981. Crystal Lake was created from a portion of Cumberland Township in 1902; *Thirteenth Census of the United States, 1910, Population of Counties*, p. 565. The *Cumberland Herald*, 30 May 1883, noted, "An organ grinder and small girl tambourine players are discoursing sweet music about town." These persons could have been early Italian settlers or traveling musicians who wandered throughout Wisconsin after 1870.

[9] Ambrose DeGidio, interview with author, Cumberland, 27 August 1981; Henry Cotone, interview with author, Cumberland, 30 August 1981.

come to Cumberland. In 1900 the city's 112 adult Italian males had lived in the United States for an average of 12.5 years, 57 of them for 13 or more years. The 105 adult Italian women averaged 10.5 years in the United States, 53 of them 11 or more years.[10]

Unlike other contemporary Italian communities, Cumberland drew comparatively few single male immigrants, and boarders were a rarity in the city's Italian homes. Census data suggest that many of the Italians who traveled to Cumberland were settlers with families, not itinerant workers. The 35 Italians listed in the 1885 Wisconsin census included 11 females, and the state census of 1895 enumerated 289 Italians, 44 percent of whom were females. In 1905 the Wisconsin census counted 662 Italians in Cumberland, comprising 266 adults evenly divided between the sexes and 396 children, most of whom were born in Wisconsin or elsewhere in the United States.[11]

The availability of jobs and inexpensive land drew Italians to the Island City. In Italy many of them had owned or leased small plots of land or were agricultural laborers. In Wisconsin they bought land and became part-time farmers, but drew much of their early income from railroad work. Indeed, the Immigration Commission found that agriculture was an "incidental occupation" until the Italians' land was paid for. The commission further noted that "paying for land with supplementary earnings from industrial labor is not new, but there are few more pronounced types of this on a community scale than that presented by the Cumberland colony." The 1900 U.S. census listed the major occupations of the settlement's 107 adult males as follows: 36 percent day laborers, 33 percent farmers, 7 percent farm laborers, and 18 percent railroad workers. Thirteen of the teenage boys worked as day laborers or on the railroad. The high percentage of day laborers probably included men who worked at a local lumber mill, on city road and construction jobs, and perhaps a few lumberjacks. The railroad workers were sent out on construction jobs to North Dakota, Montana, Idaho, Washington, and even British Columbia. For example, 57 Italians left Cumberland in April 1896 to work at railroad sites in Minnesota and Montana.[12]

---

[10] Rudolph J. Vecoli, interview with author, St. Paul, Minn., 29 August 1981; Gordon, *History of Barron County*, p. 572; U.S. Manuscript Census, 1900.

[11] Wisconsin Manuscript Census, 1895, 1905.

[12] U.S. Manuscript Census, 1900; Lee Ranallo, interview with author, Cumberland, 28 August 1981; *Cumberland Advocate*, 23 April 1896, p. 1; *Recent Immigrants in Agriculture*, p. 40.

In 1900 the Italians averaged 9 months of the year on these jobs; the average rose to 9.5 months in 1905. During the winter months, the men cleared stumps on their farm plots in Cumberland. Pay for the railroad laborers was estimated at a maximum of $1.75 per day. The boys who worked alongside their fathers and older brothers were often water boys; some of them—like Louis St. Angelo—were only eleven. By 1905 the occupations of Cumberland's Italians were more concentrated in farming and railroading. Of the 117 male adults, 50 percent were farmers, 4 percent were farm laborers, 27 percent were railroad workers, and 6 percent were laborers. Many of the men worked from five to twenty years on the railroads before becoming full-time farmers.[13]

The Italians bought land in 10-, 20-, or 40-acre lots. In 1903, the 60 Italian landowners in Cumberland and 53 of their *paesani* in the adjacent township of Crystal Lake owned a total of 4,447 acres, for an average of 39 acres per owner. In 1914, 118 owners held 5,817 acres, an average of 49 acres per owner. The parcels in Crystal Lake, which included 37 percent of the Italian population, averaged 46 acres in 1903 and 59 in 1914, while the Cumberland parcels averaged 33 and 40 acres in those two years.[14]

The Cumberland farmland was mostly cut-over forest, and farmers had to remove the stumps before planting crops. Many lots included clumps of trees that were cut for firewood. The amount of land cultivated was small at first, but gradually expanded as more stumps were removed each year. Much of the work was done by women and children. Extended families pooled the labor of the women, children and older men, who plowed, hoed, and harvested each family's land as a group. Crops included peas, beans, "pickles," potatoes, and rutabagas. Each family had a garden that produced a year's worth of vegetables for their consumption. Many of the farms had horses, pigs, and chickens, and eventually a large part of the acreage provided grazing land for the larger animals. Several Italian families raised corn and wheat as feed for their animals.[15]

Word of the Cumberland colony, one of the few Italian agricultural

[13] Wisconsin Manuscript Census, 1905; George St. Angelo, "The St. Angelo Family" (undated ms., personal papers, Lee Ranallo), pp. 8, 11.

[14] *Atlas of Barron County* (1903); *Atlas and Farmers' Directory of Barron County* (1914).

[15] Interviews with local residents, Cumberland, 27–31 August 1981.

communities in the Midwest, spread. Arminio Conte, the Italian consular agent for Wisconsin and Iowa, told the Milwaukee *Catholic Citizen* in 1909 of the "ideal Italian colony in Cumberland." However, at the same time, investigators from the U.S. Immigration Commission were reaching a far different conclusion about the Italian farm community. The commission report, published in 1911, was a mixture of fact, opinion, and generality that was often contradictory and consistently colored by a negative view of southern and eastern Europeans. Cumberland Italians were described as "foreign, clannish, ignorant, superstitious, suspicious, ill-tempered, untruthful, untrustworthy, and prone toward fighting, wielding knives and thievery." The Abruzzese farmers were characterized as "backward" and "inefficient."[16]

The commission concluded that the Italian farms were very small, but its investigators surveyed only fifty Italian farms in the Cumberland section of the colony and ignored the adjacent Crystal Lake settlement, which included more than a third of the Italian population and half the landowners. Had the full Italian population been studied, the size of the typical farm could have been greater than the thirty-six acres reported in the survey.[17]

Scandinavian employers told the investigators that Italian farm laborers required strict supervision and were not satisfactory. However, the report, in one of its few positive statements, described the men in the Italian settlement as being industrious and good workers.[18]

Italians were accused in the report of not being "actual farmers" and were described as "backward agriculturally" and inefficient in comparison to Scandinavian and German dairy farmers. The report stated that the Italians "introduced no new plants or methods of farming into the neighborhood." Yet, Cumberland's Italians have long been proud of introducing sweet and hot peppers into the area, and they report that in the past Scandinavian and German neighbors approached Italian farmers for the excellent pepper and tomato seedlings that they cultivated in their small "hotboxes" (cold frames) during

---

[16] *Catholic Citizen* (Milwaukee), 11 December 1909, p. 3; *Recent Immigrants in Agriculture*, pp. 412–13, 422, 424. For insightful comments on the preconceived notions, research methods, and statistics of the Immigration Commission, see Stephen Steinberg, *The Ethnic Myth: Race, Ethnicity and Class in America* (New York, 1981); and Oscar Handlin, *Race and Nationality in American Life* (Boston, 1957).

[17] *Recent Immigrants in Agriculture*, p. 418.

[18] *Recent Immigrants in Agriculture*, pp. 420, 422, 424.

the chilly northern Wisconsin spring.[19]

The commission report also decried the fact that many Italian men were away for nine months each year working as railroad section hands while their wives, children, and elders cultivated only a small portion of their land. Yet the commission did not look at the strategy behind this practice. The Italians wanted just enough farmland to provide food and some income for the family while the men accumulated savings from railroad work that eventually would pay for an expanded farm. During their yearly three-month break from track work, the men continued clearing tree stumps from their land, thus expanding the amount of tillable acreage.

The private side of life did not escape the commission's attention. The frame houses were described in the report as "dirty, poorly painted, and cheap" and the interiors as "slovenly, untidy, and disorderly." The report noted that Italian women were inefficient housekeepers and poor cooks who had the audacity to work outdoors "with bare feet and bare heads." Because of these traits, the report continued, Italian girls worked infrequently as domestics. Yet the 1905 Wisconsin census indicates that 17 of the 43 Italian youths working outside the home were female domestic workers. One elderly man explained that Italian families would brag that their daughters were house cleaners in the homes of Cumberland's Scandinavian "big shots."[20]

The commission report even took a stand on the Italians' eating habits, contradicting itself in the process. The *Abruzzesi* and *Calabresi* lived on vegetables and pasta until they could afford to raise hogs— a thrifty and industrious plan. The commission report criticized the Italians on the one hand for not including meat in their diet, and praised them on the other for eating a greater variety of food than other Cumberland ethnic groups.[21]

The commission noted that "of the several immigrant races that settled in the township, the Italian only are 'foreign'; they alone seem to preserve a strong race consciousness." The investigators found that the Italian colony was "rather sneeringly referred to by most men in

---

[19] *Recent Immigrants in Agriculture*, p. 424; Henry Cotone, interview with author.

[20] *Recent Immigrants in Agriculture*, p. 424; Henry Cotone, interview with author; Wisconsin Manuscript Census, 1905.

[21] *Recent Immigrants in Agriculture*, p. 420.

Cumberland." What the report did not mention was that the Italians banded together because of the sneering discrimination they faced. Early Italian arrivals encountered employment agents who promised work, collected $5 to $10 fees, and sent them out to bogus railroad jobs. When the jobs were real, as many as twenty-four men were packed into a small boxcar crammed with bunks. In other instances, Italians were hired to work for the winter in lumber camps and paid with scrip that was supposedly redeemable at the company's office in a nearby city. At the end of the season the immigrants traveled to the city only to discover that the company office was nonexistent and the scrip worthless. Incidents such as these quite naturally caused Italians to be "suspicious," as the report described them, and to respond with their own "untruthful" and "untrustworthy" attitude when dealing with non-Italians.[22]

In 1898, an event that should have prompted interethnic cooperation instead reinforced mistrust and isolation in the Italian community. A large forest fire burned out many Cumberland farmers, including a number of Italians. Shortly afterward a non-Italian woman collected money for the victims and gave it to the needy Italian farmers. She was ostracized by other non-Italians for this act, and as a result the infuriated Italians formed their own mutual aid society to avoid this type of humiliation in future times of need.[23]

Cumberland officials reported to the Immigration Commission investigators that the Italians were "rather hard to deal with politically," as American and Italian customs often clashed. In 1893 town officials passed health laws to prevent the Italians from housing people and farm animals together—a common practice in Italy. During a diphtheria epidemic that same year the town toughened its laws to prevent Italians from gathering in large groups to mourn over the bodies of victims, and invoked fines to enforce a special quarantine in the Italian settlement.[24]

The commission accused Italians of being "prone toward fighting" and "wielding knives." When violent acts did occur among Italians, the *Cumberland Advocate* was quick to dramatize the situations. In

---

[22] St. Angelo, "The St. Angelo Family," p. 3; Cumberland Centennial Committee, *Cumberland*, pp. 30–31; *Recent Immigrants in Agriculture*, p. 424.

[23] *Cumberland Advocate*, 8 October 1898.

[24] *Recent Immigrants in Agriculture*, p. 424; *Cumberland Advocate*, 23 February 1893, p. 1.

The San Antonio di Abate Mutual Aid Society in Cumberland, ca. 1910. Photo courtesy of Cumberland Public Library.

an 1891 article entitled "A Fiendish Italian," the paper reported that one Italian woman stabbed another to death, "settling the trouble existing between them in true Italian fashion, and proceeded to carve her according to the rules and regulations of the Mafia." In 1910 the newspapers echoed nativist sentiments by declaring that "assassination is not an Anglo-Saxon vice," but rather, "it is confined to our alien population that oozes through the Ellis Island gates from the Far East, the Near East, and the Latin countries."[25]

Bigotry, discrimination, and confrontation are often present when different ethnic groups encounter each other. The Immigration Commission, along with many other American institutions of that era, viewed these phenomena from a nativist position and saw the "inferior" Mediterranean race as the causal factor. The nineteen pages devoted to Cumberland in the commission report include only one observation from an Italian—a brief quote from Deputy Sheriff Sam Palmer. The entire situation might have looked different if more Italians had been interviewed.[26]

The work of the commission's field researchers may have had an immediate effect on the naturalization of Cumberland's Italian immigrants. The commission report stated that "many have been induced to take out first papers, a few are citizens, both because someone put forth some effort to bring this about." Perhaps the person referred to was the community's leader, Sam Palmer, who in 1901 became the second Italian naturalized in Barron County. Palmer was one of only nine Italians naturalized before 1909, the year of the commission's investigation. However, twenty-four Italians became U.S. citizens in 1909. This figure represents 23 percent of all Italian naturalization papers filed in Barron County between 1893 and 1954. Perhaps the commission's critical survey persuaded Palmer to encourage these Italians to become citizens.[27]

Swedes, Norwegians, and Germans in Cumberland labeled the Italian settlement "Dago Bend" and "Spaghetti Avenue," and Italians

---

[25] *Recent Immigrants in Agriculture*, p. 413; *Cumberland Advocate*, 9 April 1891, p. 2, 24 February 1910, p. 8.

[26] The commission report does mention "interviews with a fairly large number of Italian families," but only in relation to ascertaining the landholdings of early Italian settlers. If those interviewed were asked about other matters this information was omitted from the report. See *Recent Immigrants in Agriculture*, p. 413.

[27] Naturalization File, Barron County Courthouse, Barron, Wis.

were expected to stay south of Highway 63. Italian school boys in
elementary schools often fought Scandinavian youths in the school
yard. George St. Angelo, who entered Cumberland High School in
the fall of 1908, left six weeks later. He writes: "the reason—I could
not accept the ridicule and the harsh physical hazing that I was sub-
jected to by the big town boys who delighted in taking care of the
'country dago kid.'" The commission report noted that few Italian
youngsters entered Cumberland High School, and none ever graduated from the school, which was "within easy reach of the children
of the settlement." Apparently the investigators never spoke with
George St. Angelo and other Italians who could have provided an
alternative view.[28]

Interethnic encounters were not confined to the school yard. In
one incident a small Italian man was beaten by a burly Swede who
reportedly threw the Italian out of a tavern. The insulted and enraged
Italian went home and returned with a knife. The non-Italians saw
the knifing as a barbarous act, while the Italian colony applauded one
of its own who had upheld his honor by confronting a bully.

While the strict ethnic segregation in Cumberland township ag-
gravated intergroup tensions, outlying areas were sometimes characterized by greater ethnic harmony. George Ricci, born in Sprague
township in 1900, wrote of good relations between neighboring Scandinavian and Italian farmers, and noted that half of his playmates
were non-Italian boys.[29]

By the end of the first decade of this century most of the Italian
families in Cumberland had moved from their original dwellings—
railroad shanties and log cabins—into frame houses. After some difficult times in the 1890s, the small Italian communities in Cumberland
and Crystal Lake had achieved a modest degree of stability. A strong
sense of community was apparent in the institutions created by the
immigrants: St. Anthony's church in 1885, the St. Anthony Mutual
Aid Society in the 1890s, and the San Nicola Savoia di San Polo
Matese Society formed in Crystal Lake in 1912. Both of the societies
built meeting halls, and they had a combined membership of 225

[28] Henry Cotone, interview with author; George DeDominces, interview with author, Cumberland, 28 August 1981; Sam Donatelle, interview with author, Cumberland, 31 August 1981; St. Angelo, "The St. Angelo Family," p. 18; *Recent
Immigrants in Agriculture*, p. 424.

[29] George DeDominces, interview with author; George Ricci, *I Lead A Charmed
Life* (no publisher or place listed, 1974–75), p. 11.

men. Dances, social events, and community meetings were scheduled
regularly, and processions marked the annual celebrations in honor
of St. Anthony in January and Our Lady of Mount Carmel in August. Cumberland was served intermittently by Italian priests before
1920.[30]

Several Italians achieved prominence in the community. Sam
Palmer established a construction company and later became a deputy
sheriff whose work was praised in the Immigration Commission report. In 1888 Sabatino Donatelle opened a grocery store that today
is run by his grandson, Sam. A number of the American-born Italians rose from their jobs as water boys on the railroad track gangs
to the position of timekeeper, a job that offered more prestige and
power than that of track laborer, the position most of the immigrants
held. Among the second-generation leaders was Thomas St. Angelo,
a businessman and two-term office holder in the state legislature.
Amadeo Alphonse, like St. Angelo, started out as a railroad timekeeper, then managed the railroad company store, became an officer
in the Catholic Knights, and was looked up to as an advisor in the
Italian community.[31]

The Immigration Commission report did predict that Cumberland's Italians would eventually establish a stable farming community.
During the World War I era several canneries and processing plants
were established, and this encouraged the cultivation of cash crops. A
number of second-generation Italians, such as the five sons of Andigue
Ranallo, set up their own farms during this period. As the average
size of Italian agricultural plots increased, some families eventually
acquired large farms. However, the 1920s brought hardship for those
attempting to establish a farm or to maintain a business in Cumberland City. As young Italians of the postwar era matured, they found
an economy that could not support them. The family farms were often
too small to accommodate the numerous offspring of the immigrants.
Indeed, by 1930 Wisconsin's Italians had the largest family size of any
ethnic group—an average of 4.79 persons, compared to the statewide
average of 3.52 persons. There were few jobs in Cumberland, and

[30] Cumberland Centennial Committee, *Cumberland*, p. 32; Heming, *Catholic Church*, p. 858; Ambrose DeGidio, interview with author; George DeDominces, interview with author.

[31] Sam Donatelle, interview with author; St. Angelo, "The St. Angelo Family," pp. 8–9; Gordon, *History of Barron County*, p. 571.

some Italians who owned small businesses had to leave the area. In the early 1920s, for instance, Florento and Angelo DeAngelo closed their shoe repair shop and moved to California. They were followed by Pasquale Sirianni and his family, who had operated a grocery business in the Island City. Another Cumberland resident, George Ricci, graduated from 6th grade in 1916 and immediately went to work in Cumberland at the W.C. Pressing Canning Company, often putting in 60 hours per week. While World War I brought plenty of employment opportunities, the postwar years found Ricci migrating to short-term railroad, road building, cannery and steel mill jobs throughout northern Wisconsin and Minnesota. In 1923 he was married in Cumberland and moved to St. Paul, Minnesota, where he worked in a foundry.[32]

The onset of the Depression undercut any remaining potential for economic self-sufficiency, as is illustrated by the experience of Dominic DiNucci. DiNucci, the son of an early immigrant, decided that twenty years of seasonal railroad work and part-time farming were enough. He purchased 260 acres of farmland and 60 acres of woods just north of Cumberland. DiNucci cultivated a variety of crops, kept twenty-five dairy cows, and sold firewood to other Italian families. However, a three-year drought that began in 1933 destroyed his venture.[33]

Drought and the Depression discouraged many young adults in Cumberland, Italians and non-Italians alike, from farming. One indication of this is the decline in the percentage of Italians living in rural Wisconsin, from 39 percent in 1910 to 17 percent in 1930. Many young people left Cumberland to find work in larger cities such as St. Paul. People who graduated from Cumberland High School in the 1930s and 1940s report that most of their classmates left Cumberland. The onset of World War II further accelerated this migration from farms to distant cities. While the city of Cumberland's population remained constant, the combined population of Cumberland and Crystal Lake townships, where the bulk of Italians were located, fell from 2,505 in 1920 to 2,077 in 1940, and to 1,762 by 1950.[34]

---

[32] Untitled ms., Italian File, Cumberland Library, pp. 7, 13; Ricci, *Charmed Life*, p. 15; *Fifteenth Census of the United States, 1930*, Wisconsin supplement, pp. 85–86.

[33] Tom DiNucci, interview with author, Cumberland, 30 August 1981.

[34] Sam Donatelle, interview with author; Joe Alphonse, interview with author, Cumberland, 30 August 1981; Tom DiNucci, interview with author; U.S. Census, 1910, 1920, 1930, 1940, 1950 Wisconsin supplements. For 1930 the 17 percent of Wisconsin Italian Americans living in rural areas were classified as follows: 10.7

Economic and social factors created other problems between the two world wars. Competition for scarce jobs caused tension between young Italians and Scandinavians. Competition for spouses further complicated matters—many local Italians girls were marrying *paesani* who traveled from St. Paul to find wives. Highway 63 still served as a rigid social barrier—Italians were expected to stay to the south. Young men who crossed the line to date non-Italian girls were often involved in fights at dance halls and saloons. While there was some interethnic dating before 1940, cultural and religious differences kept intermarriage to a minimum. According to one Swedish woman, Scandinavian parents objected more to the Italians' Catholic religion than to their ethnic background.[35]

While World War II brought about a migration of young people from Cumberland, it also brought Italians and other nationalities together as equals in the military, and afforded an opportunity to see the world outside rural Wisconsin. Many Italians married women of different ethnic backgrounds, and after the war interethnic marriage became common in Cumberland. One man reports that the dance hall fights after 1945 were based on competition between people from different towns, not on ethnic differences.[36]

The servicemen who returned to Cumberland and other young Italians were not interested in the ethnic institutions created by their fathers and grandfathers. The St. Nicholas Society stopped meeting in the 1930s, and the larger St. Anthony's Society disbanded in the postwar years. St. Anthony's Church discontinued its religious processions and other uniquely Italian practices. Today, St. Anthony's is a multi-ethnic parish that serves as the center for the general Catholic community in Cumberland. While individual Italians maintain ethnic customs and a pride in their history, there do not appear to be any "Italian" institutions today in Cumberland.

Italians who remained in Cumberland prospered in local business ventures, especially auto repair shops and dealerships. In 1981 four of the city's eight aldermen were Italian Americans. Italians had become a respected part of the Cumberland community. As one indication of

---

percent nonfarm, 6.2 percent farm. No such breakdown was provided in earlier censuses.

[35] Tom DiNucci, interview with author; Gen DiNucci, interview with author, Cumberland, 30 August 1981.

[36] Tom DiNucci, interview with author.

this acceptance, one Italian cited the hot peppers that were introduced by his grandparents' generation. Not only have Cumberland's
non-Italians come to accept hot peppers in their diet, but, indeed,
Scandinavian Americans are sometimes the finalists in the hot-pepper
eating contest at the town's Rutabaga Festival.[37]

Cumberland's young people continued to leave to seek educational
and occupational opportunities in urban areas. A handful of Italian
American farmers operated large farms, but most Italians now had
urban trades. A number of second-generation Italians have returned
to Cumberland for their retirement years, and some third- and fourth-
generation Italian Americans now have summer homes there.

In Cumberland the Abruzzese and Calabrese immigrants cleverly
took advantage of an opportunity to avoid urban ghetto life and to
achieve economic self-sufficiency via part-time farming and railroad
work. The Italians adapted Old World agricultural practices to the
American environment and created a hybrid farming style that proved
successful for them. The Cumberland agricultural community represented a transitional stage for resourceful Italian immigrants, who secured an economic base and fulfilled the dream of owning land. These
southern Italians were probably not adept at dairy farming, and they
did not entertain grand notions of becoming large-scale farmers. Although Italian farms in Cumberland were criticized by the Immigration Commission as being small, poor facsimiles of American dairy
farms, they provided an economic base for the family, while allow-
ing immigrant men and their older sons to draw significant income
from seasonal railroad work. When this innovative economic scheme
stopped working in the 1920s, Italians again adjusted to economic im-
peratives and joined the exodus from rural to urban areas that characterized this period of American history. Like so many other Italians,
the *Abruzzesi* and *Calabresi* of Cumberland knew how to adapt and
survive, both in the Old Country and in the United States.

---

[37] Tony Cifaldi, interview with author, Cumberland, 29 August 1981; Tom Di-
Nucci, interview with author.

Little Italy: A Casualty of Time in Duluth

Jacqueline Rocchio Moran

The first Italian immigrants to make an appearance in Duluth arrived aboard a Great Lakes steamer in September 1869. Assuming that the "swarthy, colorful and good natured" Mediterraneans were the vanguard of Italian settlement in the sparsely populated village, a local newspaper enthusiastically reported their arrival and basked in the knowledge that news of Duluth's "fame and greatness" had traveled as far as the shores of sunny Italy.[1] To the probable chagrin of city fathers, the unidentified band of Italians apparently left the area before the 1870 census survey, leaving behind no other record of their existence.

By 1880, the population of Duluth was on the upswing, and the arrival that year of the first permanent Italian settlers went unnoted. Duluth was an area of second settlement for that first immigrant family, Lombards from the province of Como who had emigrated to Winnipeg in the mid-1870s. Their settlement in Duluth set off a chain reaction of primary immigration which brought some thirty families

[1] *Duluth Minnesotian*, 11 September 1869.

from neighboring villages in the Lago Maggiore vicinity over the next three decades. The Lombards eventually established themselves in houses five or six blocks north and west of the commercial district in downtown Duluth. Although they lived in fairly close proximity to one another, their numbers in the neighborhood were not large enough to constitute an identifiably ethnic community.

None of the Lombards who arrived between 1880 and 1900 was directly involved in lumbering, shipping, or railroading—the three industries primarily responsible for the twenty-fold increase in Duluth's population during that period. The majority entered the work force as masons, one-third of whom eventually turned to merchandising as an easier and more profitable way to make a living. They were mainly proprietors of small fruit, tobacco, and confectionery shops which catered to the general public. Roughly half of these shops were located on or near the main downtown business street. Most began and ended as shoestring operations, relying heavily on credit extended by non-Italian wholesalers.

On the heels of the Lombards came a significantly larger number of southern Italian immigrants. Small bands of men began arriving in the early 1880s, many of them from the sister towns of Boiano and Civita in the Compobasso region. *Paesani* from those two mountain villages eventually outnumbered all other Italians in town, although there were also large numbers of natives of other villages within 100 miles of Naples and also Calabrians from Reggio and Catanzaro.

By the 1890s, the southerners had begun to reside in homes or boardinghouses within walking distance of Rice's Point, where railroads, lumberyards, and docks were located. The purchase in 1905 of a small French church on 11th Avenue West and Superior Street cemented ties to the area—known as "the Glen"—and established the neighborhood around St. Peter's Italian Church as Duluth's most visible Little Italy. The Glen dwellers, together with the Lombards, numbered approximately 200 families at the peak of the immigration era.

The locations of two other Italian colonies which emerged by 1915 were related to the availability of jobs in the vicinity. In the mid-1890s, a grocer and a confectioner from the downtown area led the settlement of a second predominantly southern Italian colony in the newly incorporated suburb of West Duluth. This was not, strictly speaking, a satellite colony, since most of the families who settled there had migrated from other parts of the country. By 1914, when an Italian national parish was founded on 59th Avenue West and Raleigh Street, there were more than fifty Italian families in the community, most of them located close to the bayfront metal and manufacturing plants where a majority of the men worked.

A third group of Italians was drawn to the western suburb of Gary-New Duluth by the construction of a steel plant in 1914. The opening of U.S. Steel's Wire Mill Division in 1921 brought additional Italians, increasing the total to approximately fifty families. The Gary-New Duluthians were primarily northern Italians from the regions of Friuli and Piedmont. The largest number by far were from the towns of Pordenone and Cordenons in Udine, a province of Friuli. The migratory path of a number of the *Friulani* led from Michigan's copper country to a Wisconsin cheese factory owned by Chicago consul Giulio Bolognesi and Duluth consular agent Attilio Castigliano, and from there to Gary-New Duluth.[2]

It must be emphasized that the settlement of Italians within the three major neighborhoods never approached a ghettolike concentration. The West Duluthians lived in harmony with their more numerous Yugoslav neighbors, who were in the majority even in the Italian-organized parish church. The Gary-New Duluthians coexisted happily with a decided majority of Serbs, Croats, and Slovenes. Even in the 11th Avenue West Glen area, the neighborhood generally perceived as Little Italy by Italians and non-Italians alike, census tracts indicate a heterogeneous population dominated by Finns and Swedes, who outnumbered Italians roughly six to one.

Nevertheless, the clustering of Italians on certain blocks within these neighborhoods and the existence of numerous small businesses catering primarily to an Italian clientele provided self-sufficiency and contributed to a sense of community. This was particularly true in the Glen area, where Italian grocers were sometimes grouped three or more to a block, and an array of enterprises ranging from saloons to coal vendors provided essential goods, services, and social centers.

Although there was some interaction between the Glen Italians and their former neighbors living in the Raleigh Street area, geographic and linguistic differences effectively isolated the three major Italian communities from one another. In the downtown area, where south-

---

[2] U.S. Bureau of the Census, *Sixteenth Census of the United States, 1940*, vol. 2, *Statistics for Census Tracts*, Duluth, Minn. (Washington, D.C., 1942), p. 14.

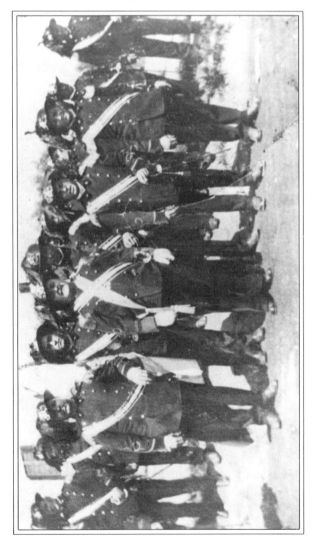

West Duluth *Bersaglieri*, ca. 1921. Photo courtesy of Kenneth Moran.

ern Italians and Lombards lived less than a mile apart, socioeconomic and dialect differences discouraged socializing, but both groups came together for worship at St. Peter's. Prior to the purchase of that church in 1905, all Duluth Italians had attended Sacred Heart Cathedral, where they met apart from the general congregation and were listed separately in the church directory. The Italians may have preferred their exclusive status within the church body, but a number of examples, both documented and undocumented, point to discrimination against the Italians by diocesan clergy and their Hibernian parishioners. Monsignor John Zarrilli's forty-year battle with his Irish superiors over the redesignation of St. Peter's Italian Church as a geographically bounded parish is a story in itself.[3]

The sacred traditions of both regional groups were preserved within St. Peter's. The Lombards, for example, were in charge of the annual festival dedicated to their favorite celestial patron, San Pietro, and the southern Italians organized the yearly celebration honoring San Rocco, the patron saint of Neapolitans. The more popular of the two was the mid-August tribute to "St. Rock." The outdoor celebration featured music by the Sons of Italy Band, keno and other games, including a greased pole contest, and handicrafts, door prizes, and numerous food delicacies. But the carnivallike atmosphere was a pale imitation of the traditional saint's day celebrations found in large and less acculturated Italian communities across the United States. The failure of the Duluth Italians to recreate the raucous *festa* processions traditional in their native villages remains unexplained. It may not be too farfetched to imagine that the pageants had been vetoed by the patriarchal Zarrilli, who was ever sensitive to possible scorn directed against him and his flock by the American church.

In 1927, the Lombards and a few southern Italian merchants provided the impetus for the construction of a new St. Peter's in a more ethnically mixed neighborhood about five blocks away. The handsome new structure was designed and constructed by the Italians themselves at great sacrifice of time and labor on the part of every member of the community. Even the large stones for the building's exterior were quarried by the Italians from the gabbro-bound hills north of the church and skidded down to the building site on sleds.

---

[3] Jacqueline Rocchio Moran, "The Italian-Americans of Duluth" (M.A. thesis, University of Minnesota, Duluth, 1979), pp. 62–84.

The new church, like the old, remained at the center of the community's spiritual and social life.

In pre-World War I Duluth, most of the Italians were absorbed into an economy generally receptive to an influx of skilled and unskilled immigrant labor. Times were lean during seasonal layoffs and periods of economic depression, of course, but the Italians fared no worse than other foreign-born residents, who constituted more than 60 percent of Duluth's population at the turn of the century.[4]

A large number of the Glen-area Italians were employed in the maintenance and cleaning of railroad cars at the Northern Pacific roundhouse or in track maintenance throughout the city. Before its demise in 1927, more than fifty Italian men and women were employed at the F.A. Patrick Company, a West End garment manufacturer whose work force was dominated by Jews and Italians. Italians were employed there in every capacity, from hand finishers to supervisors. Other typical occupations included gardening, construction, and stevedoring. A number of Italians gained a foothold in city park and street departments while working on WPA-financed projects during the Depression. A significant number of second-generation Italians living east of West Duluth or Gary-New Duluth found work at the steel fabricating and manufacturing plants located in those communities, but few of their fathers worked there.

A 1924 survey of all employed Italians indicated considerable mobility within the working classes.[5] Advancement within the seniority system was notable in the iron and steel industries, where numerous Italian laborers progressed to skilled and supervisory positions.

Commercial enterprise was the major vehicle for economic mobility out of the working class. A large number of second-generation Duluth Italians have prospered as owners of businesses ranging from corner grocery stores or taverns to multimillion-dollar food or lubricant industries. Two or three families are alleged to have made modest fortunes bootlegging during Prohibition.

Many second-generation Italians, both northern and southern, became white-collar workers via correspondence courses in bookkeeping and accounting. Among the progeny of Italian immigrant fam-

---

[4] U.S. Immigration Commission, *Reports of the Immigration Commission*, vol. 1, *Abstracts*, 61st Cong., 3d sess., S. Doc. no. 747 (Washington, D.C., 1911), pp. 150–53.

[5] Moran, "Italian-Americans," p. 43.

ilies in Duluth, only one, a Lombard, is actually a certified public accountant. The professions in general have been underrepresented among Italians in Duluth. Economic considerations may have been only partly responsible for the failure of Italian youths raised between the world wars to continue their schooling beyond the mandatory age. A Depression-era survey of enrollment at Duluth State Teachers College found the offspring of working-class, foreign-born fathers to be in the majority and the most likely to graduate.[6] Italians, however, lagged behind other European ethnics. Opportunity and motivation had increased by the time that younger children in large Italian families came to maturity in the late forties and early fifties, and a number of these individuals graduated from college and entered various professions. No studies are available to indicate whether third- and fourth-generation Italian Americans in the Duluth area have pursued higher educations to a greater or lesser degree than members of other ethnic groups, but large numbers are known to possess at least a bachelor's degree, and postgraduate degrees are not uncommon.

World War II was apparently a watershed in the history of Italian ethnicity in Duluth. According to the subjective perceptions of dozens of second- and third-generation residents, the richly divergent character of life in the Glen area had changed drastically by the time sons and grandsons of the immigrants returned from the war.

Socializing with close friends and relatives was still the favorite pastime of the gregarious Italians, but communal potato roastings, wine-pressing parties, and impromptu street-corner concerts were relegated to the past. Goats and chickens were no longer welcome in the neighborhood. The festivals had been moved indoors and transformed into staid holiday bazaars that resembled those of every other church in town. Old superstitions were discarded, even by some members of the immigrant generation, and neighborhood diviners of the cursed *malocchio* no longer held sway. Most of the beneficial societies were gone, and the Sons of Italy was no longer seen leading the mournful funeral corteges of deceased lodge brothers. In the back rooms of the few remaining stores and saloons, old cronies still gathered to gamble and gossip, but their sons no longer shot craps on the street corners. *Bocce* courts were deserted and the game was lost to memory, along

---

[6] Work Projects Administration, Project 665-71-3-218, *College Survey of Minnesota, 1926–1939* (Duluth, 1940), pp. 50–52, Duluth State Teachers College Collection, University of Minnesota, Duluth, Archives.

with the frenzied rhythms and intricate steps of the *tarantella*, once a mainstay at Italian parties and wedding receptions.

The changing character of community mores was only one step in the acculturation and assimilation of Duluth's Italian Americans. The second step was removal from the community itself. More than 75 percent of the second generation married non-Italians and established homes in neighborhoods scattered throughout town. Through the interaction of various material, sociological, and psychological forces, Italian Americans, like other European Americans, were gradually and inevitably drawn into the mainstream of life in their new neighborhoods. In time, they became more Americanized than any of the other national groups once characterized as "new immigrants." While Greeks, Serbs, Croats, Slovenes, Finns, and Jews had preserved their ethnic traditions and passed them on to succeeding generations, Italians as a community had ceased to exist. Their failure for many years to take part in Duluth's International Folk Festival was unique among ethnic groups in town.

It was partly in response to this void that a group of second-generation Italian men in their late fifties and sixties organized a new Italian-American Club in 1975. A more compelling motivation was their desire to revive a sense of community among the geographically dispersed Italians throughout town and to preserve what remained of their cultural heritage.

The club's appeal to membership based on ethnic consanguinity has not met with universal acceptance. Of the approximately 1,600 Duluthians with at least one Italian parent,[7] only 145 men and 150 women are dues-paying members of the Italian-American Club or the Women's Auxiliary, and fewer than 25 percent are active participants. Within the club, unity of interest and purpose has sometimes been lacking. A nucleus of older men with ties of kinship or lifelong association enjoy the club primarily for the social contact, while a small group of younger men would like to see more ethnically oriented activities. There are cultural as well as generational gaps. Only five or six of the central-city or West Duluth Italians can converse in an Italian dialect. The *Friulani* from the cohesive Gary-New Duluth community speak fluently their own distinctive language and continue to

---

[7] U.S. Bureau of the Census, *United States Census of Population: 1960*, vol. 1, *Characteristics of the Population*, pt. 25, Minnesota, p. 254. The 1970 census is based on the foreign-born only. Both statistics are based on a sampling.

play *bocce* with a set of balls imported from Italy years ago. A small group of newer residents from provincial Italian communities and a post-World War II immigrant family speak Italian and continue to enjoy traditional forms of recreation, such as dancing the *tarantella* or the *salterello*. Some members of this group see the locals as "not really Italian at all."

Whatever their degree of acculturation, most of the members believe that they share a common pride in their ancestry, a zest for life that includes an almost ritualistic dedication to good food and drink, and a strong attachment to family and friends. This is the real heritage that Duluth's Italian Americans will pass on to their children.

Two Little Italies
at the Head
of the Lakes

Antonio Pucci

In a recent article in the *Canadian Historical Review*, David Bercuson wrote: "They [Italian immigrants] constituted a conservative element ... . Managers welcomed Italians to the mining communities because of their excellent (or infamous?) reputation as strikebreakers. The Chinese were in much the same position. They too found Canada to be a heaven compared to what they had left. It is impossible to tell whether strikebreaking activities resulted from exclusion from unions by white workers or vice versa, but their conservative temper and exclusiveness mirrored the attitudes of many Italians."[1] Bercuson leaves the impression that the Italian Canadian immigrant of the turn of the century was a docile and submissive entity within the context of burgeoning industrial capitalism. This paper argues that the Bercuson thesis is not accurate and that it was based largely on neglect of ethnic history in Canada. In Canadian historiography we find no counterparts to such American historians as Marcus Lee

---

[1] David Jay Bercuson, "Labour Radicalism and the Western Industrial Frontier: 1897–1919," *Canadian Historical Review*, June 1977, p. 165.

Hansen, Oscar Handlin, or Rudolph Vecoli. It is only with the work of Robert Harney that the field of Canadian Italian history has been firmly established; his work has stimulated a great awakening in the fields of Canadian immigration and ethnic relations.

This paper is an attempt to demonstrate that the Bercuson thesis is unfounded, at least within the two Little Italies of Thunder Bay, Ontario.² Italian immigrants at the turn of the century in Thunder Bay are shown to be active agents in the process of change. To be sure, they responded to action, but they also initiated radical action at the workplace.

Italian immigrants began to trickle into the Thunder Bay region as early as 1883 in pursuit of railway work. Many of the original arrivals came via the United States. A letter written in 1884 by the mayor of Port Arthur to the consul general of Italy describes the arrival of a group of Italians:

> There was a large number of Italians arrived here last fall and from what I could learn they were induced to come through the persuasion of employment agents in Buffalo and other points east. On their arrival they were in [indecipherable] but were provided with provisions by the town authorities. Some of the party went east to work on the Canadian Pacific Railway a distance of one hundred miles from here, the balance left by the Sarnia steamer for Sarnia. I have not heard that any of them died from exposure but they must have suffered considerably. At the time there were [*sic*] no one here that could speak their language and consequently [they] could not make themselves understood.³

Later arrivals came to Thunder Bay after considerable experience in the United States and brought with them ideas acquired in the Little Italies of the Republic. For instance, Frank Ventrudo, who came to Fort William in 1916 after having spent four years in the United States (including a stint as a fruit vendor in the streets of Chicago) and who was one of the prime movers for the establishment of the Workers Cooperative and the Economic Cooperative in the 1920s, claimed to

---

²Fort William was incorporated as a town in 1892 and as a city in 1907. Port Arthur, about four miles east, attained city status in 1907. Together these two cities have also been known as the Twin Cities and as Lakehead. In 1970 the two were joined and given the name of Thunder Bay. Thunder Bay is also the name of the district in which the two communities are located.

³Letter from Thomas Marks, Mayor of Port Arthur, to consul general of Italy, 5 August 1884. Thomas Marks Letter Books, 1884, p. 776, Thunder Bay Historical Museum Society.

have learned the concept of a cooperative in the Italian communities of the United States.[4]

The pattern of settlement among Italians and other urban-bound immigrants was the same in Fort William as in any other North American city. Various national groups found living quarters in low-cost dwellings that were often located near the industrial plants and factories where they sought employment. These unattractive places eventually became the neighborhoods of the "foreigners." Thus, the immigrants found themselves in segregated areas first as a consequence of economic factors and second because of their desire to settle among those of similar background. In Fort William the foreigners took up residence in the shadow of their work sites in streets such as McTavish and McIntyre of the "Coal Dock Section," which eventually also became known as the East End and the Foreign Quarter. This area had become the center of the community's industry as a result of the relocation there of the Canadian Pacific Railway's operational facilities from the Westfort area.[5]

It was within the Foreign Quarter that the Little Italy of Fort William emerged among the settlements of other foreigners attracted by the Canadian Pacific Railway works and terminals and the Canadian Northern Railway. These consisted principally of coal handling facilities and merchandise or freight sheds and required plenty of men to carry out the heavy work.[6] Italians were also found in the Westfort area, but in smaller numbers. The first few Italian families there were mainly *Veneti* and *Abruzzesi*; while in the East End the Italians were mainly *Calabresi, Piemontesi, Abruzzesi, Pugliesi, Napolitani,* and *Veneti*. Most of the population of Little Italy came from the villages of southern Italy (excluding Sicily).[7]

---

[4] Frank Ventrudo (born in Orsara di Puglia, Campania, 1893), interview with author.

[5] Department of Temperance and Moral Reform of the Methodist Church and the Board of Social Service and Evangelism of the Presbyterian Church, "Report of a Preliminary and General Social Survey of Fort William" (March 1913), pp. 3–4, Thunder Bay Historical Society Archives. This and a social survey of Port Arthur were prepared by Bryce M. Stewart, who in the 1920s became Deputy Minister of Labour. These two surveys provide a wealth of information about the economic, political, and social conditions of the two communities. Hereafter cited as "Social Survey of Fort William" and "Social Survey of Port Arthur."

[6] "Evolution of the Coal Docks Section," (Fort William) *Daily Times-Journal,* 21 May 1904. It should be noted that the Italian immigrants did not use the term "Little Italy." The press and the literature of the time used the term.

[7] Tony Fogolin (born in San Vito, Udine, 1894, arrived in Fort William in 1913),

In 1904 an editorial in the local press claimed that, much like any other North American city or town of importance, Fort William also had "a corner set apart for the people of foreign birth." The article went on to say that every other city that had a working class from southern Europe also had its Little Italy in a segregated area that was shared with other non-English-speaking immigrants. The article gave no explanation of why these distinct neighborhoods had emerged, except that "it seems to be a natural condition of things that these people should segregate."[8] In Port Arthur the immigrants also lived in distinct areas of the city. The major Italian colony was located in the area between Pearl and Bay streets. However, some Italians also settled along the Fort William Road, in the area where Ontario Street and First Avenue come together.[9]

First Lessons in Industrial Struggle, 1902–1903

The foreigners began to play a role in the industrial relations of Fort William and Port Arthur in 1902. Not many details are known about these early strikes, but it would seem that it was then that the immigrants received their first valuable lessons in the despotic *modus operandi* of their employers. On 2 July 1902, a group of Italian and Finnish workers employed in the freight sheds and yards of the Canadian Northern Railway in Port Arthur asked management to increase their wages to twenty-five cents per hour. The company immediately dismissed them; the rest of the workers went on a full-scale strike on 5 July 1902.[10]

Two days later the Canadian Northern Railway responded with two powerful weapons—imported strikebreakers and armed men. Ironically, a "gang of Italians," numbering about forty men, was brought from Montreal to replace the strikers at the dock. At the same time, the company hired ten special policemen to prevent the strikers from interfering with the strikebreakers. Presented with this quick and

---

interview with author, 22 May 1974.

[8] "Evolution of the Coal Docks Section," *Daily Times-Journal*, 21 May 1904.

[9] *Social Survey of Port Arthur*, p. 4.

[10] *Daily Times-Journal*, 5 July 1902. A more detailed account of these early labor strikes is found in Antonio Pucci, "Canadian Industrialization Versus the Italian Contadini in a Decade of Brutality," in Robert F. Harney and J.V. Scarpaci, eds., *Little Italies in North America* (Toronto, 1981), pp. 183–207.

formidable response, the Italian strikers offered no counter-challenge.[11]

In 1903, Italian freight handlers employed by the Canadian Northern Railway were again the chief protagonists in the struggle against the irregular employment hiring practices at the dock. The company's policy was to hire men on a daily basis; between the arrival of vessels the dockworkers were expect to remain idle and without pay. When the workers gathered to protest on 20 May, local authorities read the Riot Act and arrested the leader; a crowd of Italian workers who had "become quite ugly" were dispersed by the police.[12] The Italians were given their pay and replaced.

In these two small confrontations the foreigners learned that the company could outmaneuver them by using strikebreakers, special private police forces that could be established at any time, and national laws enforced by local police. Nevertheless, within the next nine years the immigrant longshoremen challenged their employers three more times, with great determination and militancy.

Contadini, Violence, and Reprisal, 1906–1907

By 1905 both Fort William and Port Arthur had seen considerable economic development, but for the workers employed at the waterfront conditions were still miserable.[13] It is not surprising, therefore, that in 1906 the Italian workers staged two strikes, against the Canadian Pacific and against the Canadian Northern railways.

On 29 September, without warning, ten Italian freight handlers employed at the Canadian Pacific Railway freight sheds walked out demanding an increase in pay over the current rate of 17.5 cents per hour and 20 cents per hour for day and night work, respectively. They were also entitled to a bonus of 2.5 cents per hour, provided that they remained until the end of the navigation season.[14] Since the employers hired their workers on a day-to-day basis, the bonus system was a scheme for maintaining an abundance of cheap labor throughout the season. Even though work might be scarce at the waterfront, any worker who found work elsewhere forfeited the bonus money he had

---

[11] *Daily Times-Journal*, 7–8 July 1902.

[12] *Daily Times-Journal*, 20 May 1903.

[13] Canada, *Sessional Papers*, No. 25, "Report of R.A. Burris to the Superintendent of Immigration, Port Arthur, July 13, 1905" (1906).

[14] *Daily Times-Journal*, 1, 3 October 1906.

accumulated. In addition to the wage issue, Italians may also have been striking in response to rumors reported by the press that the railways planned to shut out Italians and replace them with "thousands of brawny English-speaking men and youths" who were expected to arrive, and by other foreigners of "sturdy races," mainly Finns, Swedes, and other Scandinavians, since they were thought to be order-loving, permanent settlers who would make "the best British citizens."[15]

On 2 October the strikers declared a general strike and instituted a blockade of Little Italy, which in essence also cut off entry to the adjacent Canadian Pacific Railway freight sheds. At 1 o'clock the *Daily Times-Journal* was distributed with the headline "Shooting and Rioting Started—New Men Coming to Take the Place of the Strikers Are Fired on by Italians." In what amounted to a small pitched battle, 2 strikers and one officer were shot when the company's superintendent arrived from Winnipeg with a carload of men who were to have replaced the strikers. Approximately 100 Italian strikers armed with guns, clubs, and revolvers awaited the arrival of the strikebreakers.[16]

However, later on the same day, four more carloads of strikebreakers were brought by the Canadian Pacific Railway from Winnipeg. Faced with the railway's reinforced special police force and no shortage of strikebreakers, the Italians called off the strike on the evening of 2 October by agreeing to a compromise worked out by the mayor. The compromise gave the workers a pay increase of 2.5 cents per hour, but nothing was done about hiring practices or the notorious practice of holding back the bonus money until the end of the season.[17]

In Port Arthur, where Italian freight handlers (many of whom commuted from Fort William's Foreign Quarter) working for the Canadian Northern Railway had walked out in sympathy for their countrymen in Fort William, the level of violence did not reach the shooting stage. However, it is interesting to note that even the Italians who were engaged on the town's excavations left work on the appeal of striking Italians, while the non-Italian workers remained at work.[18] This was surely a magnificent display of both class and group solidarity within the two Little Italies. On 2 October the Canadian Northern

---

[15] (Port Arthur) *Daily News*, 2 October 1906.

[16] *Daily Times-Journal*, 2 October 1906.

[17] *Daily Times-Journal*, 3 October 1906.

[18] *Daily News*, 1 October 1906.

Railway imported sixty-four men from Winnipeg, many of them Italians. These men had not heard of the strike. When the imported Italian strikebreakers were told of the situation by their countrymen, they, too, joined the strike. Many of the Italians who had been brought in from Winnipeg found themselves destitute and were taken care of by the Italian community.[19] Meanwhile, in light of the solidarity between the imported Italian strikebreakers and the strikers, the Canadian Northern Railway was forced to agree to a settlement similar to that of the Canadian Pacific, namely an increase of 2.5 cents per hour.

The Italians received no sympathy in the local press. A *Daily News* editorial argued that the major concern

> is the circumstance that among the strikers are a majority of foreigners, chiefly Italians, who are reported to have prepared to meet opposition to their demands at the point of the knife, the national weapon of the "dago." ... To strike for more pay is the legitimate prerogative of any man or body of men. But for a community of British citizens to have to submit to the insult and armed defiance from a disorganized horde of ignorant and low-down mongrel swash bucklers and peanut vendors is making a demand upon national pride which has no excuse.

All this was the result, the editorial argued, of a lenient policy which the community had adopted in its dealings with Italians of a "baser sort." The editor predicted that the Italians were likely to make stabbing and shooting men in the back a regular feature in industrial bargaining processes.[20]

The railway companies waited until the 1907 shipping season to shatter the moderate gains that the Italian freight handlers had won in the 1906 strikes. First came the news that, as had been rumored during the strike, the Canadian Pacific Railway was going to exclude Italians and Greeks from the freight sheds. Their work would be limited to the track lines and construction camps. They were to be replaced by 200 to 250 British workers. "Should trouble arise it is expected that the Briton will be more than a match for the Greek," the *Daily News* reported.[21] The Canadian Northern Railway struck a second blow when it announced that for the 1907 season the rate

---

[19] *Daily News*, 2 October 1906.
[20] *Daily News*, 1 October 1906.
[21] *Daily News*, 30 April 1907.

of pay would drop 2.5 cents per hour.[22]

On 10 June 1907 the British workers and other foreigners—Hungarians, Poles, and Finns—who had replaced the Italians walked out demanding higher wages. The Canadian Pacific responded by immediately rehiring the Italian and Greek workers that it had earlier locked out.[23] Here we can see that the division of the working class along ethnic lines was cultivated and exploited by management.

Troops Intervene in Little Italy, 1909

In 1909 a strike at the Canadian Pacific freight sheds commanded national attention. The conflict lasted only six days, but before it was over it took on the character of a miniature civil war between the residents of Little Italy, on the one hand, and on the other, the Canadian Pacific's special constables, the local police, the local militia, and regular troops that were dispatched to the scene from Winnipeg.

On 9 August 1909, 600 freight handlers, most of them foreign born, walked out of the Canadian Pacific sheds demanding higher wages.[24] Once again the Italians and Greeks were perceived as the instigators and leaders. On 10 August, Italians began to patrol Little Italy armed with sticks, stopping anyone who appeared to be a strikebreaker. When the railway moved thirty of its imported special constables into the area, the constables were mistaken for strikebreakers; a thirty-minute gun battle ensued.[25]

The local militia was soon brought into Little Italy. It happened that a famous Canadian military figure, Colonel S.B. Steele, was visiting the area; he decided to take personal charge of the troops and requested seventy-five regulars from Winnipeg.[26] Steele used the mili-

---

[22] *Daily News*, 4 May 1907.

[23] "Greeks and Italians Seem to Have Broken the Freight Handlers Strike" was the startling newspaper report. *Daily Times-Journal*, 11 June 1907.

[24] *Daily Times-Journal*, 9 August 1909.

[25] *Labour Gazette* 10 (September 1909): 344.

[26] Ibid., p. 344. The regulars arrived by a special train on 13 August (*Daily News*, 13 August 1909). With the involvement of Steele, the strikers were confronted with a formidable military intervention. Steele did not lack experience in mounting military operations. He had first served with the military during the Fenian Raid in 1866. In 1873 he joined the North West Mounted Police and served until 1899, except during the Riel Rebellion in 1885, when he commanded the cavalry and scouts of General Strange's column and was involved in key operations of the campaign. Steele participated in the actions of Frenchman's Butte, and as commander of the mounted force, he successfully led the pursuit and defeat of Big

tary, who had orders to shoot to kill if necessary, to seal Little Italy. In a search for weapons the police and the soldiers literally ransacked the Italian homes and outbuildings. The search uncovered about thirty revolvers and rifles. The Canadian Pacific also brought in French Canadian workers, but when these men learned of the strike, about 50 of the 100 penniless French Canadians joined the strikers.[27]

Faced with the formidable power of the company, backed by the local police and the military, the strikers held a "conference of all nations" and agreed with a proposal to have Federal Minister of Labour MacKenzie King arbitrate the dispute under terms of the Industrial Dispute Investigation Act. The investigating board awarded the strikers an increase of 3 cents per hour (making their new hourly rate 20.5 cents per hour) and recommended that the practice of retaining the bonus earned until the end of the season be abolished.[28]

At the beginning of the 1910 shipping season, the management of the Canadian Pacific took another stab at eliminating the gains made by the workers during the bloody 1909 struggle. It was announced that, as in 1907, the Italians and Greeks would no longer be given employment in the freight sheds. Even the "white Italians" (Italians from northern Italy) were included.[29]

Given the bitter context of the situation, one might have expected a forceful reaction by the excluded Italian and Greek workers. Indeed, the railway company anticipated such an occurrence and took steps to counter it. The railway brought to the city its chief secret service agent, C.H. Andrews. Andrews made it known that the strikers of the 1909 season were being replaced by 350 French Canadians from Montreal and that the railway was now in a position to thwart any disturbances, as it was well armed. In his words:

[Y]ou can bet your life that they won't make as much headway as they did last fall. The police department of the C.P.R. is organized this year, and just now enough constables could be mustered to compete

Bear's band and the Wood Crees. After 1899 he served as commander of the Lord Strathcona Horse during the Boer War, and later as chief of the South African Constabulary in the Transvaal. A short summary of Steele's career is available in Henry James Morgan, *The Canadian Men and Women of the Time*, 2d ed. (Toronto, 1912). See also Steele's autobiography, *Forty Years in Canada* (London, 1915). Unfortunately, this work covers his life only up to 1907.

[27] *Daily Times-Journal*, 14 August 1909.

[28] *Labour Gazette* 10 (September 1909): 341–347.

[29] *Daily News*, 8, 14 April 1910.

with a company of soldiers, let alone a bunch of foreigners who would not stop running if they saw a red coat walking down the coal docks streets. We don't anticipate any trouble, but should the Greeks and Italians start a riot we will be on hand.[30]

Faced with this formidable show of strength, the Italians and Greeks did not mount a challenge.

The Deprenzo Case, 1912

The last major industrial conflict prior to World War I occurred in the summer of 1912. The strike was against the Canadian Northern Coal and Ore Company. The coal handlers (many of whom were from Fort William's Foreign Quarter) had managed to form Coal Handlers Union Local No. 319. Since its inception in 1911 the union had been influenced by Italians; its first president was an Italian, Mike Pento, and its first treasurer was Nicola Ciacco.[31]

When the company was presented with the union's set of demands it responded by firing the president and the secretary. On 20 July 1912 the coal handlers set up their picket line on a strategic point in Port Arthur's Little Italy, which commanded the only entrance to the coal docks. In the evening several men attempted to cross the picket line to go to work but were turned back by the strikers, who were "flourishing" a revolver.[32]

A policeman arrived at the scene to arrest the Italian strikers, but the policeman was himself disarmed by five or six strikers who drew revolvers. Learning of this incident, the chief of police, with a number of officers, went to the scene to arrest the ringleader, a man known as "Tony the Shoemaker," but the police were met by strikers armed with clubs and guns.

A violent confrontation ensued. The police force suffered a number of injuries, and many Italians were wounded. Two Italian brothers, Dominic and Nicola Deprenzo, suffered the most extensive injuries in the ordeal. Dominic received seven bullets; Nicola was hit by five bullets and both his hands were "shot off."[33]

---

[30] *Daily Times-Journal*, 13 April 1910.
[31] Coal Handlers Union Local No. 319, Minute Book, 18 March 1911, Thunder Bay Historical Museum Society Archives.
[32] *Daily News*, 30 July 1912.
[33] Ibid.

Two Italians enjoy a game of *bocce* in Fort William's Little Italy, ca. 1912. Photo courtesy of Antonio Pucci.

The local militia moved to the scene, and squads of soldiers and police "ransacked Italian houses" searching for weapons. The search produced no weapons and resulted in no arrests.[34] The authorities offered protection to anyone who wanted to work, but none dared. The local paper reported that the company was taking no chances:

> A special squad of policemen armed with Winchester rifles with sufficient ammunition to blow the inhabitants of Port Arthur's "Little Old Italy" into eternity were soon patrolling the property of the Canadian Northern Coal and Ore Dock Company.[35]

Five days later the company accepted most of the demands, and the strike ended.

The ramifications of the strike, however, lingered on in the Italian community, and for the two Deprenzo brothers the strike had tragic consequences. Both brothers were brought to trial on 8 October 1912.[36] Dominic was charged with attempting to murder the chief of police, and Nicola was charged with assaulting a constable. To say the least, the police evidence against the two brothers was highly questionable, but the defendants did not speak English well and were less convincing witnesses.

The defense fought the case on the grounds of compassion rather than on the quality of the evidence given by the police. Their lawyer suggested to the jury that they keep in mind the circumstances of the Italian immigrants and the important role they were playing in the Canadian industrial process:

> He said they were mostly coarse, rough, uneducated peasants from southern Italy, their only advantage being their strong frames and tough sinews that made them an invaluable acquisition to Canada, for performing the rough, dirty work such as handling coal. They were, he said, the hewers of wood and drawers of water. They were thrifty and saving. Most of them had dependents away back in Italy and as each pay day came along they sent their savings to support their loved ones at home.

The judge in charge of the case saw the trial of the Deprenzo brothers as an opportunity to teach the foreigners, and particularly the Italians, a lesson:

---

[34] *Daily Times-Journal*, 31 July 1912.

[35] *Daily Times-Journal*, 1 August 1912.

[36] The following account of the trial is based on the *Daily News*'s account of the proceedings. *Daily News*, 9 October 1912.

The point he emphasized was that those foreigners must not be led to believe that they can take the law in their own hands, throwing aside the measures provided by civilized society for the punishment of crime. If this condition was once allowed civilization would descend to barbarism and anybody having a grievance would be inclined to take the law in his own hands and resort to violence and outrage to avenge his wrongs. The law would be overthrown and the courts of Justice would be a hollow mockery. The point that must be brought home to these people was that violence in any form will not be tolerated in this country, regardless of any custom or usages prevailing in Russia, Finland, Italy or whatever country the foreign element comes from.

The jury recommended that the charge of attempted murder be dropped, but found the Deprenzo brothers guilty of resisting arrest and of unlawfully wounding. Determined to teach the Italians a lesson, Judge Middleton sentenced both brothers to a prison term of ten years at Stoney Mountain Penitentiary.[37] The sentence caused a great deal of grief among workers,[38] particularly since it was common knowledge that in fact it was "Tony the Shoemaker" who hit the chief of police over the head with a pick handle. He fled the scene and was spirited into the United States by the local "Black Handers."[39]

Conclusion

These strikes suggest that the Italian immigrants' militancy and willingness to risk their lives in armed confrontations were an essential factor in their partial success. It is apparent that the violence of the Italian strikers was prompted by their employers' conduct in the bargaining process. Management's first response to a strike was almost instinctively to turn to local or imported recruits to break it. The only effective means that the Italians and other foreigners had to keep alive the possibility of winning concessions was to introduce physical force to prevent others from taking their jobs. Without the resolve to risk their lives during the introduction of strikebreakers, a strike would have been, in many cases, a lost cause from the moment it started.

During this turbulent decade of Canadian history, 1902–1912, the Italians of Fort William and Port Arthur who were at the forefront of

---

[37] *Daily News*, 10 October 1912.

[38] "Social Survey of Port Arthur," p. 8.

[39] Anthony Pento (born in Port Arthur, 1905), interview with author, 30 July 1976.

violent strikes had little or no previous experience in industrial conflict. But they faced with determination practically all of the strikebreaking schemes ever devised. Paradoxically, they too for a short time became a tool of strikebreaking in 1907. After British and other foreign workers had without challenge accepted Canadian Pacific's policy of excluding Italian labor, the Italians returned to work for the railway when those employees struck for higher wages. It should be made clear, however, that the Italians made their greatest impact in Thunder Bay as effective strikers—not as strikebreakers.

The high degree of militancy that the Italians displayed in their new proletarian roles in Thunder Bay was not a trait that originated exclusively in the new industrial milieu. Neither was this militancy an automatic application of the "revoltist traditions" that were deeply rooted in their agrarian background.[40] The militancy of the Italian immigrants was shaped by their semifeudal European past combined with the harsh industrial present that seemed to lock them into perpetual industrial serfdom, thus undermining the success of their mission to America. To quote Eric T. Hobsbawm, "But it must never be forgotten that the bulk of industrial workers in all countries began, like Americans, as first-generation immigrants from preindustrial societies, even if they never actually moved from the place in which they had been born. And like all first-generation immigrants, they looked backwards as much as forwards."[41]

The crowded conditions of the Foreign Quarter had some positive consequences. Although the lifestyle of the Foreign Quarter residents was regarded with disgust and distrust by the established Anglo-Canadian community, crowding facilitated close intragroup relationships. This led, particularly in the case of the Italians, to a high degree of class and ethnic solidarity. Although the documentation of Italian Canadian history is still sketchy, one basic view has become stuck in the popular historical consciousness—that Italian immigrants passively submitted to the harshest conditions of a burgeoning North American industrial capitalism. But the evidence presented in this

---

[40] Daniel L. Horowitz, *The Italian Labor Movement* (Cambridge, Mass., 1963), pp. 23, 327. Horowitz points out that in many preindustrial societies, protest against oppressive conditions is usually unorganized, giving rise to "revoltist traditions." In rural Italy, both in the south and in the north-central region, "revoltist traditions" were particularly entrenched.

[41] Eric J. Hobsbawm, *Primitive Rebels: Studies in Archaic Forms of Social Movement in the Nineteenth and Twentieth Centuries* (New York, 1955), p. 108.

paper clearly demonstrates that the popular generalization does not describe the Thunder Bay experience; here the Italian Canadians were at the forefront of ethnic militancy.

The outbreak of World War I halted these volatile waves of labor-capital confrontation. During the 1920s and 1930s the residents of Little Italy were almost fanatically concerned with presenting a good group image to the community at large. The aim of this strategy was to win honor the *patria* (fatherland) and, in turn, to win acceptance in their new land. It was thought that by maintaining high standards of morality these two goals could be achieved. Doing honor to the *patria* meant, of course, that residents of Little Italy generally embraced the cultural and political initiatives of Cavaliere Emilio Marino, the local *agente consolare* of Fascist Italy.[42]

An analysis of the benevolent society of Fort William's Little Italy, *Società Italiana di Benevolenza: Principe di Piemonte*, from its inception in 1909 to 1940 shows that its most important social goal was to promote the respectability of the Italian community. The society's minutes indicate that over the years the *Principe di Piemonte* fostered a sense of pride in Italian heritage and enforced a strict code of conduct for its members. The society emerged as an agent of social control within the Italian community. Given this orientation, it is not surprising that the first Italian Canadian elected to Parliament was from Fort William. Naturalized citizen and successful businessman Hubert Badanai was elected as a Liberal in 1958. He was reelected in 1962, 1963, 1965, and 1968, and retired from the House of Commons in 1972. Earlier, Badanai served as mayor of Fort William (1949–52 and 1955–58) and as alderman (1940–48).

Past militant action against the establishment was not an advantage in the effort to win acceptance within the host community. As a result, the Italians' partial strike victories did not become part of the folklore of the community. On the contrary, the author found a great deal of reluctance to discuss these events when he interviewed a number of pioneers who lived through this dramatic period.

However, the degree of militancy and its intensity over a prolonged period of time cannot be denied. Because of the impact this militancy had on Canadian industrial relations, the two Little Italies at the head of the Lakes emerge as extraordinary agents of change.

---

[42] Antonio Pucci, "The Italian Community in Fort Williams's East End in the Early Twentieth Century" (M.A. thesis, Lakehead University, 1977).

Mining Towns

Pioneer Paesani
in Globe, Arizona

Phylis Cancilla Martinelli

Globe is a mining town spread over the mountains of eastern Arizona. A huge globe of silver ore gave the town its name and defined the principal mining interest in early years. Globe was established in 1876, when persistent prospectors wrested the area from Apache control. Italians were among the residents of the then remote mining camp; the 1882 territorial census recorded eleven men from Italy.[1] Most likely they were men without families, and their stay must have been brief, because their names do not appear in later years. They probably left when the silver boom ended around 1883. Though few in number, the Italians were not unnoticed. An attempted shooting between two *paesani* was dramatically labeled an "Italian vendetta" in the local paper.[2]

The 1890s saw the ascent of copper mining and the arrival of Italian families. In 1895 the Bigando family arrived in Globe by stagecoach, which was an uncomfortable and dangerous way to travel.[3] Along

---

[1] U.S. Census Office, *Tenth Census of the United States, 1880, Arizona Territory*, Gila County (microfilm, Department of Library, Archives and Public Records, State Archives Division, Phoenix).

[2] "Vendetta," *Arizona Silver Belt*, 16 August 1880.

[3] Nick Ragus et al., eds., *Honor the Past ... Mold the Future* (Arizona, 1976), p. 75.

with other immigrant families, the Bigandos faced the double adjustment of adapting to an alien American culture while also learning to cope with the rigors of pioneer life.

In 1898 the arrival of railroad service ended the frontier era in Globe. The town became less isolated with the introduction of relatively comfortable transportation. Thus the population began to grow and change. "Foreigners" made up an increasingly large part of the population, which included Italians, Slovenians, Mexicans, Irish, Cornish, Austrians, and Chinese.[4] The Italian community really began to form at the end of the frontier period. The aim of this paper is to account for the Italian community in Globe as it existed from the turn of the century to about 1930, using a variety of methods and sources: census records; city directories and other municipal records; newspapers and other printed sources; interviews with Italians about their past experiences; and field notes with recorded conversations and observations.

The perspective for this study emerged from sociological and anthropological approaches. From Max Weber comes an early but still useful definition of an ethnic group as a group with "a subjective belief in their common descent because of similarities of physical type, or customs, or both, or because of memories of colonization or migration."[5] Weber further noted that this subjective belief in a common descent was important for the formation and continuation of communities that are based on units other than kinship.

The ethnic community in a multiethnic society such as ours gives, according to Milton Gordon, a basis for group self-identification, and forms a subnetwork of social institutions and groups.[6] This allows the individual to confine primary group interaction to the ethnic group, while still interacting in secondary group settings with the larger society. This community is not entirely formed by the desire of ethnic groups to sustain a separate identity and unique cultural patterns, but is also shaped by the prejudice of the dominant society.

The fields of sociology and anthropology are changing their perspectives about ethnicity. For a long time an assimilationist assump-

---

[4] Clara Woody, *Globe, Arizona* (Tucson, Ariz., 1977), p. 203.

[5] Max Weber, "Ethnic Groups," in Talcott Parsons, et al., eds., *Theories of Society* (Glencoe, Ill., 1961), vol. 1, p. 306.

[6] Milton M. Gordon, *Assimilation in American Life: The Role of Race, Religion and National Origins* (New York, 1964), p. 3.

tion was dominant in both fields—ethnic cultural patterns gradually eroded in an American melting pot. The study of ethnic communities in sociology was dominated by Robert E. Park and his race relations cycle, which held that total assimilation was the inevitable conclusion of the cycle.[7] Recently, varied perspectives have emerged to challenge Park, including the work of Andrew Greeley, Michael Novak, and Robert Blauner.[8] In anthropology, as Stephen Stern has noted, folklorists have used a survivalistic framework which looked for "pure" Old World cultural elements, seeing modifications of such elements as a sign of contamination rather than of adaptability.[9] This static view is now being challenged by a perspective introduced by Fredrik Barth. Barth emphasizes the subjective, dynamic aspects of ethnicity and focuses on the ways in which interaction is structured along the boundaries of ethnic groups.[10] Along the lines suggested by Barth, George De Vos has a similar interest in boundaries and in the traditions—such as language—which set members of an ethnic group apart from other groups with which they interact.[11]

The focus of this paper will be on the subjective and dynamic aspects of ethnicity, looking at the ways in which the members of Globe's Italian community set themselves apart. In particular, the significant overt signals, or diacritical features—language, food, recreation, and general lifestyle—will be explored.[12] In addition, the subnetworks formed by the community will be studied; these include mutual aid, business ties, and general socializing.

Italian Migration

Globe's Italian community was dominated by northern Italians, mostly from Piedmont, which is unusual compared to the general pattern

---

[7] Robert E. Park, *Race and Culture* (Glencoe, Ill., 1950), pp. 194–95.

[8] Andrew M. Greeley, *Ethnicity in the United States* (New York, 1974), pp. 290–317; Michael Novak, *The Rise of the Unmeltable Ethnics* (New York, 1973); Robert Blauner, "Internal Colonialism and Ghetto Revolt," *Social Problems*, Spring 1969, pp. 393–408.

[9] Stephen Stern, "Ethnic Folklore and the Folklore of Ethnicity," *Western Folklore* 36 (January 1977): 7–32.

[10] Fredrik Barth, ed., *Ethnic Groups and Boundaries* (Boston, 1969), p. 10.

[11] George De Vos, "Ethnic Pluralism: Conflict and Accommodation," in George De Vos and Lola Romanucci-Ross, eds., *Ethnic Identity, Cultural Continuities and Change* (Palo Alto, Calif., 1975), pp. 5–41.

[12] Barth, *Ethnic Groups*, p. 14.

of Italian migration to America. The main flow of Italian migration
was from southern Italy. However, there were roughly three phases of
Italian migration to the United States, and not all were predominantly
southern. The first was individualistic; explorers, artisans, merchants,
and adventurers came to the British colonies in North America.[13]
The second phase was a pioneer migration starting in the 1860s, as
increasing numbers of Italians, mainly from northern Italy, sought
their fortunes in America. The third and largest wave, which began
about 1880, eventually brought millions of southern Italians to the
United States.[14]

Poverty was the common lot of rural Italians during the period of
mass migration. However, poverty alone did not trigger the decision
to leave. As John MacDonald has pointed out, in areas with a militant
working class, such as central Italy and Apulia, the migration rate was
low despite the level of poverty in Apulia. In areas where militancy
was not strong, which included the Alps and Sicily, poverty did lead
to a decision to migrate.[15]

Piedmont had several elements which contributed to the poverty of
the rural people. In the upper reaches of the area the soil was rocky
and unproductive, making the return for farmers minimal. Most of the
people from Globe migrated from the province of Turin, where about
three-fourths of the land is mountainous and not ideal for agriculture.
Problems of deforestation in the hilly and mountainous areas also
contributed to rural poverty.[16]

A particularly salient element in Piedmontese agriculture was the
extent of the subdivision of the land. In 1881, Piedmont had the highest percentage of direct owner-cultivators in Italy.[17] The subdivision

---

[13] Giovanni Schiavo, *The Italians in America Before the Civil War* (1934; reprint
ed., New York, 1975), pp. 43–180.

[14] Robert F. Foerster, *The Italian Emigration of Our Times* (1919; reprint ed.,
New York, 1975), pp. 324–27.

[15] John S. MacDonald, "Migration versus Nonmigration: Regional Migration
Differentials in Rural Italy," in *Proceedings of the International Population Conference* (New York, 1961), pp. 491–98.

[16] William N. Beauclerk, *Rural Italy* (London, 1888), p. 112; Valerio Castronovo,
Economia e società in Piemonte dall'unità al 1914 (Milan, 1969), pp. 101–102. The
description of conditions in Piedmont is the result of suggestions, translations,
and articles from Andrew Canepa, curator of the Western Regional Chapter of
the AIHA. He also assisted in providing spellings for words in dialect. However,
any errors or omissions are the responsibility of the author.

[17] Castronovo, *Economia*, pp. 5–16.

was in part related to specialized cultivation of mulberries, fruits, and vines. Another factor was the sale of church lands by speculators who sold small plots of land to people eager to become proprietors.[18] In the period prior to World War I there were twenty-two property owners for each 100 hectares in Piedmont; half the rural population owned property. This can be contrasted with lower rates of land fragmentation in the other Alpine areas. In Lombardy there were fifteen property owners per 100 hectares, with less than a third of the rural population owning property. Even lower ratios were found in the Veneto, with thirteen property owners per 100 hectares and less than a quarter of the rural population owning property.[19] The small plots of land in Piedmont, combined with rocky, thin soil, made economic survival precarious for rural people.

Pushed by economic conditions, numerous Piedmontese and other northern Italians joined the stream of emigrants to the United States during the third phase of immigration, which was dominated by southerners. Many northerners found their way to the western states rather than the urban enclaves settled by the majority of Italian immigrants. During the greatest period of migration there was a large proportion of northern Italians in the West. For example, in 1904 the overall ratio of southern to northern migrants was 80 percent to 20 percent. However, in the West the ratio was almost reversed: 77 percent northern Italians to 23 percent southerners.[20] Andrew Rolle speculates that this was because northerners had more money on arrival.[21] So far there is no evidence that this was the case for the Piedmontese who came to Globe. Many did not come to Globe directly, but worked across country gradually.[22] They came looking for jobs, often taking several years to save money to invest in businesses. What they acquired usually came from hard labor, thrift, and an eye for advancement. One man recalled how his father, unexpectedly stalled in

---

[18] Mario Pagella, *L'evoluzione economica delle colline dell'Astigiano* (Milan, 1962), pp. 330–37; Antonio Gallenga, *Country Life in Piedmont* (London, 1858), pp. 86–94; and Foerster, *Emigration*, p. 110.

[19] Ferdinando Milone, *L'Italia nell'economica delle sue regioni* (Turin, 1958), pp. 40–42.

[20] David L. Nicandri, *Italians in Washington State: Emigration 1853–1924* (Washington State, 1978), pp. 25–26.

[21] Andrew Rolle, *The Immigrant Upraised* (Norman, Okla., 1968), pp. 95–96.

[22] Ragus, *Honor the Past*, p. 104, tells of the travels of the Bairo family through several mining camps.

Morenci, Arizona, had to save for two years before he could complete his plans to join a brother in Globe.[23]

Many of the Piedmontese who ventured to the West became involved in mining, as was the case in Globe. In the mining fields northern Italians generally outnumbered southerners.[24] While mining was not a major industry in Piedmont, as early as 1848 almost 4,000 workers were employed in that field.[25] Scattered settlements of Piedmontese could be found in mining communities in Washington, Indiana, Wyoming, Texas, Oklahoma, Utah, and Colorado.[26]

Arizona attracted a small number of Italians: in 1900, 699 Italians made up 2.9 percent of the state's foreign-born population; in 1910, 1,531 Italians constituted 3.3 percent.[27] Most were from the north; data for 1904, for example, show that 89 percent of the new Italian arrivals to Arizona were from the north and 11 percent were from the south.[28] Many of these migrants went into copper and gold mining,[29] establishing themselves in such towns as Bisbee, Jerome, Morenci, Goldconda, White Hills, and Globe. Thus, Globe's Italian community represented a small but typical rivulet in the broader stream of northern Italian migration to the West.

The Community

Physically, the Piedmontese community occupied a distinct location on the northwest side of Globe. The choice of location was influenced in part by economics, and many of Globe's ethnic groups could be found in this area. Several streets housed most of the Italian families: Euclid, Hackney, Pinal, Willow, and North Broad. A major concen-

---

[23] All interviews were conducted in Globe or Phoenix in 1980–81. Five women and four men participated in extensive interviews, and two men in shorter interviews. Many casual conversations also were recorded during visits to Globe.

[24] Eliot Lord, *The Italian in America* (New York, 1905), p. 100.

[25] Maurice F. Newfeld, *Italy: School for Awakening Countries* (Ithaca, N.Y., 1961), p. 568.

[26] Nicandri, *Italians in Washington*, p. 38; Rolle, *The Immigrant Upraised*, pp. 67, 202, 206, 228; Kenny L. Brown, *The Italians in Oklahoma* (Norman, Okla., 1980), p. 18; Antonio Mangano, *Sons of Italy* (1917; reprint ed., New York, 1972), p. 29.

[27] U.S. Bureau of the Census, *Sixteenth Census of the United States, 1940, Population*, vol. 2, *Characteristics of the Population*, Arizona, Table 15, "Foreign Born 1850–1940" (Washington, D.C., 1943), p. 363.

[28] Nicandri, *Italians in Washington*, p. 126.

[29] Foerster, *Italian Emigration*, p. 35.

tration of Italians was on Euclid Street, called *Caniùn Sale* by the Piedmontese because of the way the steep street drops down from the Pinal Mountains, and because many families were from Sale Castelnuovo (now named Castelnuovo Nigra). The high incidence of families from the same small town highlights the process of chain migration. Most people initially indicated Turin as their home, but closer questioning revealed more precise locations. Those who were not from Sale were usually from towns in the same area northeast of Turin, such as Drusacco, Rivarolo, or Castellamonte. There also were some non-Piedmontese Italian families on Euclid, and some non-Italian families as well. Of the permanent Italian families in Globe, 46 percent lived for a time on Euclid Street.[30]

An area close to Euclid Street was home to 15 percent of the Italian families; it was called "Panama," possibly because some of the men had worked on the Panama Canal before moving to Arizona.[31] Some of these families were also from the Turin area. Seventy-five percent of Globe's Italian population lived in the northwestern section of town. The remaining 25 percent were dispersed throughout the town, and several families lived on farms in nearby Russell Gulch. Although physical proximity is not necessary for an ethnic community, it does constitute a way in which an ethnic group sets itself—or is set—apart. Thus, the clustering of Italians in Globe can be seen as one dimension of the boundary of the group.

The little Italian community that formed in northwestern Globe was also set apart by its use of the Piedmontese dialect, which, while obviously different from English, was also distinct from standard Italian and from southern Italian dialects. American-born children learned the dialect from their parents, relatives, and neighbors. Sometimes the maintenance of language was a barrier to entry into the larger society. One respondent, who came to Globe from Sale at age six, recalled the difficulty of learning English in school because so many classmates spoke Piedmontese; thus it was easy for a new arrival to rely on the dialect rather than master a new language.[32] Adults who did not learn English readily found themselves dependent on their children or English-speaking *paesani* for transactions in the larger community. Seeking to avoid such dependency, some young

---

[30] Information taken from Globe city directories, 1905–1928.
[31] Interview.
[32] Interview.

men advertised for an English teacher in the local paper.[33] One advantage of being fluent in Piedmontese that many people mentioned was the ease with which they learned Spanish, a useful language in Arizona.

Besides facilitating language maintenance, living together allowed constant visiting, casual socializing, and mutual aid, and encouraged intermarriage. Occasionally kin shared the same house, as was the case with the Falbo, Faletti, and Rabogliatti brothers and their families.[34] More often, relatives lived across the street or a block away from each other, which meant ties of kinship were active. Mutual aid also flourished among unrelated neighbors or *paesani*, who helped each other during illness, childbirth, or to add a room onto a house. Among the members of the Italian community helping each other was an institution. Certain people, because of kin or regional ties, were expected to help on a regular basis. Failure to help was considered deviant, and was not forgotten.

Wine and beer making brought people together. Grapes came from Pomona or Cucamonga, California, where Piedmontese Secondo Guasti had established the Italian Vineyard Company (later taken over by a half dozen wineries using the vines he planted).[35] When the trucks arrived from California the entire west side of town was permeated with the smell of fermenting grapes. Although in later years a family might modify a washing machine to mash the grapes, in early times families often shared a more primitive press. They would run the first batch for their good wine, which was put in bottles and carefully corked. The bottles were then laid flat on a shelf to wait for guests or a special occasion. The second wine was barreled for daily use; with brown sugar added it was a lighter wine.[36] While the Piedmontese were not the only ones who made wine in Globe, wine making, because of special methods, could be seen as a dimension of the ethnic boundary. This was made clear by the characters in Mari Tomasi's novel about Piedmontese stonecutters in Vermont, who discussed how wine makers from other regions profaned wine and abused

[33] *Arizona Silver Belt*, 13 September 1906, p. 10.

[34] Western Directory Co., *Globe and Miami City Directory* (Long Beach, Calif., 1928), pp. 24, 55.

[35] Rolle, *The Immigrant Upraised*, p. 270.

[36] Interview.

their stomachs by making an inferior vintage.[37]

Beer making was also a communal effort, starting with the need to have a *crota*, or cellar, dug into the hillside or in a part of the basement. The beer was made using gunnysacks, hops from Giacoma's or Giaquinto's store, and three-pound cans of Blue Ribbon syrup extract. Once the brew was bottled it was laid at a tilt in a sandy corner of the cool cellar. Since all the Piedmontese on Euclid Street made beer, sampling the "Choc" beer was an important ritual. The men sat on benches and tasted the beer from a large porcelain cup kept on hand for that purpose. When one batch was not quite right, the group would move on to the next *crota* for another draw of beer.[38]

For the most part, the Italians' traditional enjoyment of intoxicating beverages was ignored by the larger society. However, during Prohibition Italians and federal agents disagreed over the right of the immigrants to make and occasionally sell their homemade wine and beer. One resident remembered that a federal agent raided the Piedmontese community, smashing so many wine barrels that Pinal Street ran red with wine, and leaving some without their *vino* for a time.[39] Violating the Prohibition laws was not the exclusive domain of Globe's Italians. The Piedmontese and other Italians in the coal mining areas of Oklahoma battled liquor laws as early as 1907. They claimed their "Chocktaw" or "Choc" beer (possibly the source of the name for Globe's beer) was essential to their health because of the bad water in the mining camps. Their arguments were ignored; between 1907 and 1930 the majority of criminal charges against Italians in Krebs and other towns in Oklahoma involved minor liquor violations.[40]

The homes in which the Piedmontese lived in *Caniùn Sale* and Panama were modest wooden buildings, typically surrounded by flourishing gardens. Many families kept cows and produced enough milk to sell the surplus; some families eventually went into the dairy business. The gardens had all kinds of vegetables, such as lettuce, artichokes, celery, and squash, with fig and peach trees providing shade and fruit. The bounty from the gardens provided welcome fresh accompaniments to meals and allowed the families to save a fair amount

---

[37] Mari Tomasi, *Like Lesser Gods* (Milwaukee, Wis., 1949), p. 140.

[38] Interview.

[39] Interview.

[40] Brown, *Italians in Oklahoma*, p. 64.

of money. For immigrants these savings were important. As Jean Scarpaci has pointed out, Sicilian laborers in Louisiana were able to save most of their meager earnings and go into their own businesses because they were good gardeners and made much of their own pasta, cheese, bread, and clothing.[41] This self-sufficiency was also typical of the Italians of Globe.

The meals eaten by Italian families were generally little modified by American cuisine. Just as the immigrant tongue had difficulty shaping itself to make the sounds of a new language, the immigrant palate had difficulty adapting to the taste of new foods. Food preferences are a function of culture;[42] as distinctive foods become associated with a certain group, they become part of the boundaries which set off a community. Filling yet economical dishes from Old Country recipes graced the tables on Euclid Street. Soups were made with turnip greens, chestnuts, or *vermicelli; polenta* made from a special blend of corn meals was a dinner staple or a snack for children when filled with cheese and baked. In addition to a variety of pasta dishes, Piedmontese *agnulòt (ravioli)* were prepared with meat for special occasions or Christmas. *Bagna cauda*, a heated dip for vegetables, was a favorite dish. *Sausissa* (sausage) was made at home and provided another occasion for families to join forces. *Merlus* (dried cod) also appeared on the Italian table.

Occupations

To meet their special food requirements, it is not surprising that some immigrants went into the grocery business, supplying items such as *polenta* and dried cod, which could not be grown at home and were too exotic for the average grocery store. Dominic Zucco and Company, with partners John Ranier and John Bono, owned a grocery store that catered to Italians. Zucco and Company were known for their willingness to help their countrymen through hard times by extending credit or being generous in their transactions. Angelo Martimbianco, who ran a grocery store and butcher shop, delivered meat to Italian families. Others who owned grocery stores were Simon Abell, Barney Morello, Bert Vidano, and Gaetano Maletta. The peripatetic Louis

---

[41] Jean A. Scarpaci, *Italian Immigrants in Louisiana's Sugar Parishes* (New York, 1981), p. 131.

[42] Robert Bierstedt, *The Social Order* (New York, 1970), p. 133.

Rosasco, who from his home in Prescott delivered Italian groceries to many Arizona communities, also delivered orders in Globe. Solomon and Wickersham also carried goods for Italians, and imported certain items, such as *antipasto*. The store stocked *macaroni* and tomato paste in twenty-pound boxes and *polenta* in ten-pound cloth bags; pigs' feet and olives were sold in bulk. Dried cod and breakfast cheeses were sold to families in wooden boxes. Deliveries were made to families in town as well as to miners living in the mountains.[43] The Arizona Bakery, run by several Italian families, starting with Dominick Revello, provided fresh bread for those who did not bake their own, rounding out the food needs of the community.

Some stores also carried herbs and other items used in home remedies. Whiskey and linseed poultices were used as preventives during flu epidemics. Children swallowed a spoonful of white cod liver oil to ensure good health. However, the most ubiquitous remedy was *camomilla*. Like *La Tonietta*, the fictional Piedmontese "doctor" and midwife who carried dried chamomile buds and little else in her medical bag, the Piedmontese of Globe relied on the beneficial effects of the mild flower.[44]

Another occupation that served the Italian community was running a boardinghouse for the many single immigrant men, mostly miners. For the homesick immigrant the boardinghouse environment, "with its wine- and smoked-filled atmosphere, so similar to the sounds and smells of the homeland, provided reassurance and allayed anxieties in a strange, new land."[45] Globe had several boardinghouses for Italians, often run by widows, for the work was equated with keeping house and was therefore acceptable for women. Thus, when Anna Vidano Ranier's second husband died she opened a rooming house, as she had done before in Chandler, Colorado.[46] Married women might take in boarders to add to their husbands' paychecks or to help out in difficult times. When her husband was injured in the mines, Frances Chiono took in boarders.[47] Women also took in laundry, did sewing, and sometimes helped out in their husbands' stores. Several Italian

---

[43] Interview.

[44] Mari Tomasi, *Deep Grow the Roots* (New York, 1940), p. 69.

[45] Rolle, *The Immigrant Upraised*, p. 140.

[46] Interview.

[47] Interview.

women worked for the Arizona Steam Laundry. However, most women were kept busy at home.

Another business venture popular among members of the Italian community was running a saloon. The ethnic saloons in Globe and other mining towns were social centers where "men discussed their day's labor, talked local and national politics, and speculated about the future of the mines and their community."[48] The saloons owned by partners from Piedmont, Constantino Giacoma and James Bracco, were an excellent example of the multiple purposes served by this business in the ethnic community. Starting out with the Fashion and Big T saloons, they soon expanded to the Fashion Building in 1909. The lower floor of the cement-block building was occupied by the Fashion Cafe and Bar, which served both drinks and meals. The upper floor was designed as a lodge hall and was rented out for meetings, dances, and other social events. There were also rooms to rent and a *bocce* court.[49]

The saloons catered to miners; the majority of immigrants were engaged in mine work. Most worked at the Old Dominion mine, which dominated Globe. Some men had mining experience in Italy, possibly at the copper mine near Traversella, Piedmont. The immigrants worked as laborers, muckers, millmen, quarrymen, and miners in the Old Dominion. Work in the mines was difficult and dangerous; many young immigrant men were buried in the Globe cemetery, instead of returning to Italy with a fortune.

Alice Hamilton, a doctor investigating health problems related to mining, described her visit to the Old Dominion.

> We stepped into a "cage," which is a flimsy, shaky elevator, devoid of walls or anything else one can cling to, and dropped down into darkness ... in ... the Old Dominion, we dropped eight hundred feet, and that seemed a long way .... I trudged along, stooping to avoid overhangs, ... scrambling on hands and knees ... climbing down an eighty-foot ladder into a black pit, and worst of all, crossing deep pits on rails which were so far apart I felt sure I could fall between them if I slipped.[50]

Hamilton concluded that, while working with drilling-machine jackhammers might produce health injuries because of vibrations, the

---

[48] Ronald C. Brown, *Hard Rock Miners* (College Station, Tex., 1979), p. 46.

[49] Interview.

[50] Alice Hamilton, *Exploring the Dangerous Trades* (Boston, 1942), pp. 216–17.

A general store in Globe, ca. 1900. Photo courtesy of Phylis Cancilla Martinelli.

most immediate threat to the miners was the dust produced by the hammers. Indeed, black lung or miner's consumption claimed many lives. Lives were also lost to injuries. Occasionally, serious accidents would injure several Italians who were working together; the 1906 explosion at the Old Dominion involved four *paesani*.[51]

Globe was the center of labor activity in Arizona. The city saw the inception of mining unions in the territory, and became a symbol for other mining areas in the state. Neither the Industrial Workers of the World nor the mining companies were able to wrest control from the local International Union of Mine, Mill, and Smelter Workers.[52] Unfortunately, at this point little has been uncovered about union activity among the Italians. Respondents do recall that some Italians were involved in union activity, but no names have surfaced. The Fashion Saloon was known as "a union establishment, ... largely patronized by the union men."[53] Perhaps the lack of information is because many of the more outspoken union men may have left Globe after the celebrated 1917 strike. The demands of copper miners in Arizona during the war years were considered unpatriotic. While the Bisbee deportation of IWW members in July 1917 attracted the most attention, in Globe the IUMMSW and IWW were caught up in a struggle that involved both violence and peer pressure.[54] Mine owners were reluctant to take back striking miners, feeling it would be unfair to workers who had not struck. Settled in October 1917, the strike left lasting scars. Hamilton described the bitterness still felt in Globe in 1919, noting that the majority of the miners she spoke to had come to town after the 1917 strike.[55] Thus, the lack of information on union activity among Italians does not rule out the possibility of their involvement, but offers an interesting area for future research.

Many Italian miners disliked working underground because of the danger and because there were often conflicts between the Italians and the "Cousin Jacks," or Cornish miners. The Cousin Jacks were in supervisory positions, but through skill and hard work Italians of-

---

[51] *Arizona Silver Belt*, 25 January 1906, p. 1.

[52] James Ward Byrkit, "Life and Labor in Arizona, 1902–1921: With Particular Reference to the Deportations of 1917" (Ph.D. diss., Claremont Graduate School, 1972), p. 87.

[53] "The Fashion Building," *The Border*, February 1909, p. 21.

[54] Michael E. Casillas, *Mexicans, Labor and Strife in Arizona, 1896–1917* (M.A. thesis, University of New Mexico, 1979), p. 113.

[55] Hamilton, *Exploring*, p. 218.

ten challenged Cornish superiority. These elements combined to make many leave the mines as soon as they could. Joseph Cubitto, a watchmaker by trade, worked in Utah coal mines and Globe copper mines before saving enough to open a small watchmaker's shop, which today is Globe's oldest continuous business. Felix Bertino, a tailor in Piedmont, labored in Arizona mines for ten years before leaving Globe to start farming in Phoenix.[56] Walter Tocco also left for farm life, while Dominick Faletti went into contracting. Frank Dalmolin became a brakeman for the Arizona Eastern Railroad, which employed several Italians. The Rabogliatti brothers, Steve, Domenick, and Alfred, became entrepreneurs. They left mining for the saloon business; when Prohibition threatened, they saw the potential for movies. They opened several theaters and eventually invested widely in real estate.[57] Some Italians brought to Globe skills they used immediately. John Caceletto, a shoemaker in Piedmont and France, began repairing the hobnailed shoes of Globe miners. Several Italians went into this business, including Frank Cavalieri, Bob Valerio, Dominic and Steve Vernetti, and Gaetano Maletta.

The Italians of Globe patronized each other's businesses, worked together, and relaxed together. *Bocce*, card games such as *briscola*, and *morra*, a guessing game played with outflung fingers and a lot of emotion, filled many hours. Weekend dances were popular family affairs; they began because Italians were not welcomed at dances of other groups. The weekly dances were held at the lodge hall or in Giacoma's storage building. The big dances sponsored by the *Lega Fratellanza* on the Fourth of July and Columbus Day were especially festive. The *Lega Fratellanza* is perhaps the best known of the Globe Italian clubs. Founded in December 1905, it was a mutual benefit society affiliated with the Columbian Federation of Italian American Societies. The *Lega* provided inexpensive sickness and death benefit insurance. It also loosely linked Globe Italians to Italians in other Arizona towns, such as Jerome.[58] There were other short-lived Italian clubs; the Italian Masonic Lodge and the Italian Progressive Society both met at the Miners' Union Hall.[59]

---

[56] Phylis Cancilla Martinelli, "Italy in Phoenix," *Journal of Arizona History*, Autumn 1977, pp. 319–40.

[57] Interview.

[58] Interview.

[59] Walsh and Fitzgerald, *Globe and Miami City Directory 1916–17* (Phoenix, 1916), p. 10.

Families gathered for picnics at Wheatfield or other pleasant spots out of town. In addition to their abundant food, the picnics are remembered for the music of Rico Troglio and others. An accordion or harmonica played *Chiribiribin* or *La Violetta*, bringing back Italy for a moment. Some Piedmontese held a special picnic in June in honor of Saint John. This points out a division within the community: some Globe Italians were Catholic, while many were strongly anticlerical, an attitude often found in northern Italy. Religious celebrations therefore were not focal events, as was the case in other Italian American communities.

Music infused the community in other ways. A local Italian band played for dances, weddings, and funeral processions. Impromptu concerts after work were given by miners, with familiar melodies filtering through Euclid Street. In later years many Italian boys joined the harmonica band, which played at social events.

Plans for one special celebration in 1927 fell through, but the event brought the local Italian community together and remains a vivid memory. When Italian aviator Francesco De Pinedo made a historic three-continent flight, his flight plan took him near Globe. He landed on the waters of Roosevelt Lake, formed by the world's largest granite-block dam, which Italian workers helped build. An explosion sank the plane. Italy's Fascist government claimed sabotage, but De Pinedo himself denied the claim.[60] Although De Pinedo met with members of the Italian community, the celebration was canceled.

Conclusion

A researcher arriving in Globe today would find little of the historical Italian community. Only a few of the old Italian families remain on Euclid Street. Most of the families remaining in Globe have moved to nicer residential settings, in areas where few Italians once lived. The Old Dominion mine has closed, and mining no longer provides an economic focus for Globe. Many younger people have left the town to earn a living, and many have married out of their ethnic group. The *Lega Fratellanza* still exists and provides services to its members. However, for some these services are no longer sufficient. The small amount sent by the *Lega* for burial services, for example, does not begin to cover today's expenses.

---

[60] *Arizona Silver Belt*, 5–7 April 1927.

Detailed research would be necessary to determine the extent to which ethnicity remains salient for Globe's Italian American community. However, one aspect is still easily observed. As Georg Simmel pointed out, a society is also made up of "an immeasurable number of less conspicuous forms of relationship and kinds of interaction."[61] For Globe's Italian community, gossip within the ethnic community and intimate nicknames used by the Italians, such as "Checo" or "Pantalone" for the fellow with the baggy pants, created minor ethnic boundaries. In Globe today, these minor boundaries can still be found. People keep close track of members of the Italian community even if they have moved away. Nicknames are still used, and gossip, humorous stories, and news of births, weddings, illness, and death still circulate. The community exists, although in a form rather different from its early period.

---

[61] Kurt H. Wolff, *The Sociology of Georg Simmel* (New York, 1950), p. 9.

Italians on the Gogebic Iron Range

Paul A. Sturgul

The Gogebic Iron Range is one of many in the Lake Superior region. The Gogebic lies 25 to 30 miles south of Lake Superior, partly in Wisconsin and partly in Michigan. It is 80 miles long and seldom more than half a mile wide. Most of the population is located in a narrow band centering on the twin cities of Ironwood, Michigan, and Hurley, Wisconsin. In 1980, the total population of Gogebic County, Michigan, and Iron County, Wisconsin, was less than 30,000; but in 1920, at the peak of the iron mining activity on the Range, there were nearly 50,000 people living in the two counties.[1]

When settlement of the Gogebic Range began in 1884, it drew much of its population from the older, established mining communities of the Lake Superior region. These areas had already developed a mixed population which served as a prototype for the new communities of the Gogebic. The population of the older communities included Cornish, Irish, Slavic, Scandinavian, Finnish, and Italian immigrants. Most of the Italians came to the Range as miners—as did the other immigrants—but some also came with the railroads, as did my ma-

---

[1] H.R. Aldrich, *The Geology of the Gogebic Iron Range of Wisconsin* (Madison, Wis., 1929), p. 5; Lawrence Martin, *The Physical Geography of Wisconsin* (Madison, 1932), pp. 375–82; U.S. Census Bureau, *Fourteenth Census of the United States, 1920, 1980 Census of Population.*

ternal grandfather, who arrived in northern Wisconsin in 1884. My grandfather was born in Calabria, but nearly all of the early Italian settlers on the Range came from northern Italy and Austria.[2] Primarily from the Tyrol, Piedmont, and Veneto, these northern Italians also included immigrants from Bergamo and Brescia in Lombardy, Udine, the Marches, Tuscany, and Corsica. The Tyroleans, one of the largest groups, at first considered themselves Austrians rather than Italians, since their ruler in the Old Country was the Emperor Franz Joseph and not King Vittorio Emanuele.[3] The Tyroleans, along with northern Italians from the Piedmont and Veneto, came to the Gogebic Range by way of mining areas outside the Lake Superior region, such as the Illinois and Pennsylvania coal fields and the copper mining area of Montana. At first there was considerable movement among these regions as economic conditions fluctuated on the Range. For example, Hurley's Italian-language newspaper, *La Nostra Terra*, reported in 1913 that "Peter Martini of Carey left for Coal City, Illinois, where he has decided to locate permanently." Five years later, however, Martini was listed in a local directory as the proprietor of Martini's Meats and Groceries in Hurley.[4]

Italian immigrants also came to the Gogebic from other parts of Europe. A large group came to Iron Belt, Wisconsin, from Calais, France, where Italians had been employed to build the harbor; others arrived from Kassel, Germany, where they had worked in the coal and steel industry; still others, including Louis Neda, editor of *La Nostra Terra*, came to Hurley from South America.[5]

The northern Italians settled in all of the Range communities, but their largest concentration was in Hurley. At first, except for a small number of Calabrians and Sicilians, there were few southern Italians

---

[2] U.S. Immigration Commission, *Reports of the Immigration Commission*, vol. 16, *Immigrants in Industries: Pt. 18, Iron Ore Mining*, 61st Cong., 2d sess., S. Doc. no. 633 (Washington, D.C., 1911), p. 404.

[3] Much of the information in this paper is from interviews conducted between September 1975 and October 1981 with the following persons: Paul Alfonsi, Mary Astor, James Flandrena, Pauline Boretti Hausworth, Louis Lopez, John J. Prospero, and Katharine Samuelli, Hurley, Wis.; Mary Gentile Brost and Warren Buccanero, Iron Belt, Wis.; James Kaffine, Pence, Wis.; and Domenic Santini, Ironwood, Mich.

[4] *La Nostra Terra*, 1 March 1913, p. 1; *Polk's Directory of Hurley-Ironwood, 1917–1918* (Chicago, 1917), p. 19.

[5] *La Nostra Terra*, 8 March 1913, p. 1. See also *Ironwood Daily Globe*, 9 October 1963, p. 2.

on the Range. After the turn of the century, however, Italians from the provinces south of Rome began arriving on the Gogebic.[6] Most of them were from the Abruzzi, with smaller numbers from Sicily, Calabria, and Puglia. The southern Italians settled primarily in Hurley and Ironwood, with few on the western Gogebic Range. The community of Pence, for example, located four miles west of Hurley, was overwhelmingly composed of Tyrolese, Piedmontese, and Corsicans.[7] By 1910, the number of southern Italians in Hurley approached that of northern Italians; ten years later, there were as many southern Italians—mainly Abruzzese—as there were northern Italians.[8]

The Italians came to the Gogebic Range because of the availability of jobs in the iron ore mines. The 1911 report of the U.S. Immigration Commission concluded that the mining companies needed workers from southern and eastern Europe to do the "low type" of unskilled labor demanded by the "unprecedented development of the mining industry in the Lake Superior Region." The commission also noted that the industry policy following labor strikes not to "employ, when they could avoid it, the [strike] leaders ... tended to the greater employment of the Italians and other more recent immigrants."[9] Some southern Italians may also have arrived on the Gogebic as strikebreakers. This happened on the Mesabi Iron Range in Minnesota and in Michigan's copper mining area, but it is not known to what extent it occurred on the Gogebic.[10] By 1911, Italians ranked second only to Finns in population and constituted almost 30 percent of the Range's total work force.[11]

Although most Italians came to the Range to work in the iron mines, many soon moved into mercantile occupations. In Iron Belt, Wisconsin, sixteen of the thirty business establishments in 1913 were operated by Italians. With the exception of three grocery stores, these were saloons.[12] Italians also began to take advantage of the political

---

[6] U.S. Immigration Commission, *Iron Ore Mining*, p. 404.

[7] Ed Marolla, "Anton Endrizzi, Mayor of Pence," (Milwaukee) *Italian Leader*, July 1934, p. 4.

[8] *St. Mary Parish Jubilee Souvenir Record Book* (Hurley, 1936), pp. 38–39.

[9] U.S. Immigration Commission, *Iron Ore Mining*, pp. 410–11.

[10] Hyman Berman, "Education for Work and Labor Solidarity: The Immigrant Miners and Radicalism on the Mesabi Range" (1963, ms. copy in Immigration History Research Center, University of Minnesota), p. 43; William Gates, *Michigan Copper and Boston Dollars* (Cambridge, 1955), pp. 130–33.

[11] U.S. Immigration Commission, *Iron Ore Mining*, p. 404.

[12] *Wisconsin State Gazetteer, 1911–1912* (Chicago, 1911), p. 431.

opportunities made available by their numbers. By the mid-1890s, ten years after settlement of the Range began, Italians had entered public life and in a number of instances had been elected to office. Already in 1895, a Venetian, Joseph Chiono of Hurley, was serving as Iron County commissioner. In 1898, Tyrolean Joseph Brighenti of Iron Belt was elected Iron County clerk of court. In 1898, Charles Bonino, a Piedmontese, was elected sheriff of Iron County, and in 1900 he became chairman of the township of Vaughn, which includes the city of Hurley. In 1920, the first person elected judge for Iron County was James Flandrena, also Piedmontese. Three of his six successors have been Italians.[13] Thus, the Italians on the Gogebic Range became the first of their nationality to hold county and municipal office in Wisconsin. This trend continued, and by the 1930s, Italians from the Gogebic were being elected to the state legislature. In 1932, Paul Alfonsi, a school teacher from Pence, was elected to the Wisconsin Assembly on the Progressive Party ticket. In 1938, Alfonsi, who was of Corsican descent, became assembly speaker; in 1940 he ran unsuccessfully for governor. Alfonsi served for nearly thirty years in the Wisconsin legislature.[14]

Italians also sought opportunities in banking. In 1920, the aforementioned Charles Bonino, the most prominent Italian on the Range, founded Hurley National Bank. The *Montreal River Miner* reported that opening-day deposits totaled $86,000. The bank, known locally as the "Italian bank," prospered during the 1920s. Bonino, however, was not to become another Giannini. When Hurley National Bank failed on 24 June 1932, Italians lost considerable amounts of money, some their life savings. During the 1920s some Italians were stockholders in Hurley's Iron Exchange Bank. Many of these families survived the financial reverses of the Depression in good condition. Having made their fortune in Hurley, a few returned to Italy to live and married their daughters off to "titles." Today, a large block of stock in the Iron Exchange Bank is owned by the Caldabini family, who returned to Italy following their daughters' graduation from high school.[15]

---

[13] Work Projects Administration, *History of Iron County*, Historical Project no. 6555 (Hurley, 1938), pp. 17, 24; letter from Otto Erspamer, Hurley, to John Gentile, Iron County sheriff, Hurley, 3 July 1970, Otto Erspamer Papers, Iron County Historical Society, Hurley.

[14] *Wisconsin Blue Book* (Madison), 1933, p. 237, 1941, p. 487; interviews.

[15] Work Projects Administration, *History of Iron County*, pp. 154–55; *Montreal River Miner*, 26 March 1920, p. 1; Iron Exchange Bank, Hurley, "List of

In addition to participating in the business and political life of the Range, the Italians formed numerous mutual aid societies. A 1901 directory lists two Italian societies in Hurley, the Italian Mutual Society and the Riflemen of Savoy, and there is evidence of others in Hurley and elsewhere on the Range. The *Società Unita Austriaca Tirolese de Benevolenza*, for example, is recorded in a 1901 civil case in Iron County Circuit Court. The society had retained the services of one Julius Patek to organize a celebration honoring the birthday of the Emperor Franz Joseph. A dispute over payment for Patek's services arose, and he sued the society. The court ruled in Patek's favor but reduced the amount of damages sought, on the grounds that the band supplied by Patek did not play "into the evening" as expected by the society. A list of twelve Italian societies of Iron County compiled in 1938 by the Work Projects Administration included *Mutuo Soccorso*, founded in Hurley in 1892; the Benevolent of Quattro Abruzzi, organized in 1905; the Italian Women's Society, the Garibaldi Club, and the Speranza Society from Pence. Today only the Quattro Abruzzi survives as an annual-dinner club for Italian men.[16]

At one time these societies played an active role in the Italian community and participated in funerals and *festas*. Their biggest celebration, though, was on Columbus Day. Early in the development of the Italian community Columbus Day became an occasion for the display of both American patriotism and Italian pride. The 1909 celebration, organized by the six Italian societies of Hurley, was announced by the *Montreal River Miner* as

> the biggest event ever undertaken by the Italian residents of the Range. The parade will be one of the chief features of the celebration and will be participated in by all of the Italian societies of the Range in their regalia and several fraternal organizations. The Hurley and Norrie bands will furnish music all day. A large float has been constructed representing the *Santa Maria*, Columbus' flag ship .... [T]he parade will be through the principal streets of Hurley and Ironwood and on its return will go to the Hurley ball park where the representation of the landing of Columbus will be enacted .... [A]n elaborate dinner will be served at the Burton Hotel at one dollar per plate. In the evening the grand ball will be given at Bonino's Hall.[17]

Stockholders," private memorandum, 1921; interviews.

[16] *Wright's Directory of Hurley and Ironwood, 1901–1902* (Milwaukee, 1901), p. 171; *Julius Patek v. Società Unita Austrica Tirolese de Benevolenza*, Iron County Circuit Court, Hurley.

[17] *Montreal River Miner*, 8 October 1909.

Columbus Day celebration in Hurley, 1911. Italian immigrants portray (left to right) aide to Uncle Sam, Uncle Sam, Pocahontas, Queen Isabella, King Ferdinand, and Columbus. Photo courtesy of Paul A. Sturgul.

The Italians also made their presence known on the Range through their membership and participation in the Catholic church. Although most of the early Catholic population on the Range was not Italian but Irish, French Canadian, Polish, and Scotch, the first pastor of St. Mary's parish of Hurley was an Italian, Father Gilbert Nuonno. Nuonno was born near Genoa and came to the United States as a Franciscan priest in 1866. Father Gilbert, as he was commonly known, served as Hurley's pastor from 1877 until his death in 1908. In 1906, on the occasion of the dedication of the cornerstone of St. Mary's Church, Archbishop De Medio Falconio, the apostolic delegate to the United States and Nuonno's college classmate, came to Hurley. The parish jubilee book regarded Falconio's visit as "the most memorable event in the history of the Parish."[18]

Despite the presence of an Italian pastor, however, parish life in Hurley and elsewhere on the Range was dominated for many years by non-Italians, especially the Irish. Not until 1914 did Italian women belong to St. Mary's Altar Society. Religious observance was low among the Italians, especially those from southern Italy. Only the Tyroleans, who came from Austria and did not share in the estrangement between church and state of the *Risorgimento*, had no anticlerical feelings when they arrived on the Range. Early in the twentieth century, the Presbyterians and Methodists attempted to capitalize on Italian anticlericalism. Their conversion efforts were also inspired by a desire to clean up the allegedly lawless conditions on the Range, especially in Hurley, which had early become known as "the Hell-hole of the Range."[19] "The four toughest places in the world are Cumberland, Hayward, Hurley, and Hell," it was said at the time, and Hurley was the toughest of all. Hurley's reputation for crime and bawdiness led novelist Edna Ferber to choose it as the setting for *Come and Get It*.[20] Evidence of the clean-up effort may be seen in a notice from the Hurley Methodist Episcopal Church that appeared in the *Iron County News* in 1906: "The need in Hurley is great ... indeed we have looked to the Lord for Hurley, with its sins and its neglected conditions, with breaking hearts ever since we first knew of it."[21]

---

[18] *St. Mary Jubilee Book*, pp. 25, 27.

[19] Work Projects Administration, *Michigan: A Guide to the Wolverine State* (New York, 1941).

[20] Work Projects Administration, *Wisconsin: A Guide to the Badger State* (Chicago, 1940), p. 374.

[21] *Iron County News*, 21 January 1906, p. 5.

Soon thereafter the Methodists dispatched the Reverend De Simone to the Gogebic Italians. De Simone was soon followed by the Reverend Theodore Boretti, who was sent to Hurley from New York by the Presbyterians. The Presbyterian Synod of Wisconsin had high hopes for its conversion efforts on the Range:

> The Rev. T. Boretti, the Italian minister, is meeting with success among his people on the Range. Twenty-five Italians are now enrolled as members of the Hurley Church. The service of Mr. Boretti is demanded by the Draft Board as a speaker for public gatherings of all kinds. The best Italian families of the community are backing up the parish work with great enthusiasm.[22]

However, very few Gogebic Italians became Protestants as a result of the efforts of the Presbyterians and Methodists. Boretti, who married an Italian Waldensian, eventually stopped preaching in Italian at the Presbyterian church and devoted his time to the steamship ticket and insurance business. In that capacity, he was looked up to by the other Italians.

As the Range Italians became more Americanized, anticlericalism greatly diminished. The first Italian from the Range to become a priest was Father Anthony Righino of Hurley. Righino was born in Taganrogg, Russia, which had been settled by merchants from Pisa in the fourteenth century, and came to the Gogebic to live with an uncle in 1920. A number of other men and women entered religious life, including several from southern Italian families.[23] Today, Italians are active in parish life on the Range at all levels.

By 1920, settlement of the Gogebic Range was complete. Restrictive immigration laws and the end of boom times on the Range ended most of the opportunities for settling the region, not only for the Italians but for other ethnic groups as well. Between 1920 and 1960 the number of people living in Iron County decreased by 25 percent, while the decline from 1960 to 1970, the period during which iron mining ceased, was even more dramatic—nearly 20 percent in Iron and Gogebic counties.[24] Although mining still provides nearly a thousand jobs at the White Pine Copper Company in nearby Ontonogan County,

---

[22] The Presbyterian Synod of Wisconsin, "The Gogebic Range Parish," *Minutes of the Synod of Wisconsin* (Madison, 1918), pp. 25–26.

[23] *St. Mary Jubilee Book*, p. 40; *St. Mary Parish Diamond Jubilee Souvenir Record Book* (Hurley, 1961), pp. 49–51.

[24] U.S. Bureau of the Census, *Fourteenth Census of the United States, 1920, 1960 Census of Population, 1970 Census of Population.*

the mining industry no longer dominates the Range's economy. Today, the main source of income on the Range is Social Security.

Because Italians came to the Gogebic in such large numbers, however, both in absolute and relative terms, their presence on the Gogebic has remained strong. Located in a sparsely settled region, isolated from large cities, and unaffected by population infusions from elsewhere, the Gogebic Italians have retained their group identity and given the Range a distinctive character, setting it apart from the rest of Wisconsin.

Italians

on Minnesota's

Iron Range*

Rudolph J. Vecoli

Minnesota has not attracted many Italians as permanent residents. Of the more than two million Italian immigrants who arrived between 1899 and 1910, fewer than 10,000 designated Minnesota as their destination. The state's Italian-born population peaked in 1910 at 9,668 and has since declined. In 1970, of the more than four million first- and second-generation Italian Americans in the country, only 12,910 lived in Minnesota.[1] Yet many tens of thousands of Italian workers did come to Minnesota, labored here a few months or years, and then left. Thus the state does figure in the biographies of a much greater percentage of the Italian immigrants than the above figures would suggest.

---

* This paper is based on the author's article, "The Italians," in June Holmquist, ed., *They Chose Minnesota: A Study of the State's Ethnic Groups* (St. Paul, 1981), pp. 449–71.

[1] U.S. Bureau of the Census, *1970 Census of Population: General Social and Economic Characteristics, United States Summary* (Washington, D.C., 1972), Tables 144, 145; U.S. Immigration Commission, *Reports of the Immigration Commission*, vol. 3, *Statistical Review of Immigration, 1820–1910*, 61st Cong., 3d sess., S. Doc. no. 756 (Washington, D.C., 1911), p. 210.

Italians were drawn to Minnesota by two forms of employment: railroad work and iron mining. Northern Minnesota's iron ore deposits were not exploited until the late nineteenth century—the Vermilion Range in 1884, the Mesabi in 1892, and the Cuyuna not until 1911. The expansion of these mining operations coincided with the growing influx of southern and eastern Europeans and attracted many of them to Minnesota. Northern Minnesota thus became the unlikely location of the largest concentration of Italians in the state. By 1890, the towns of Tower and Ely on the Vermilion Range each had about one hundred Italians. But the Mesabi, with its rich surface deposits, quickly overshadowed the Vermilion. By 1909, Italians constituted 10 percent of the labor force of the Oliver Iron Mining Company, the subsidiary of U.S. Steel which dominated the industry. The great majority of these Italians were on the Mesabi Range. In 1910, there were more than 4,000 Italians (roughly 40 percent of the state's total) in St. Louis and Itasca counties, the iron mining region.[2]

Along with the Cornishmen, Swedes, and Finns, the first Italians to arrive on Minnesota's Iron Range came from the Upper Peninsula of Michigan and northeastern Wisconsin. Since the 1860s, Italians had worked in the copper and iron mines there. Northern Italians— Piedmontese, Lombards, Venetians, and Tyrolese (then "Austrians") —predominated on the Upper Peninsula. Immigrants from Abruzzi-Molise, Campania, Calabria, and Sicily arrived later, particularly after 1900. Step migration from the Upper Peninsula can be documented from parish records as well as from contemporary accounts and oral interviews. Marriage records of the Church of the Immaculate Conception of Eveleth, for example, frequently list Vulcan, Iron Mountain, and Bessemer, Michigan, as places of birth.

Of particular interest is the presence in northern Minnesota of immigrants from central Italy, especially the regions of Emilia-Romagna, the Marches, and Umbria, which were distinguished by their relatively low rates of emigration. Many Italian families on the Range

---

[2] Attilio Castigliano, "Origine, sviluppo, importanza ed avvenire delle colonie italiane del Nord Michigan e del Nord Minnesota," *Bollettino dell'emigrazione* no. 7 (Rome, 1913), pp. 723–39; John Syrjamaki, "The People of the Mesabi Range," *Minnesota History* 27 (September 1946): 206–208; George O. Virtue, *The Minnesota Iron Ranges*, U.S. Bureau of Labor Bulletin no. 84 (Washington, D.C., 1909), p. 347; U.S. Immigration Commission, *Reports of the Immigration Commission*, vol. 16, *Immigrants in Industries: Pt. 18, Iron Ore Mining*, 61st Cong., 2d sess., S. Doc. no. 633 (Washington, D.C., 1911), pp. 291–305.

trace their origins to these regions. Oral interviews often mention previous mining experience of fathers and grandfathers in Italy or in northern Europe. Research in provincial and communal archives in Italy has confirmed these statements. By the late nineteenth century, immigrants from Sassoferrato, a small *paese* in the Appenines of the Marches, were leaving for both Luxembourg and the United States. A few kilometers from Sassoferrato were the sulfur mines of Cabernari and Rotondo. Those emigrating were often experienced miners who left to work in mines elsewhere. The same pattern can be observed from the sulfur mines of Boratella Terza in Romagna and the lignite mines in the vicinity of Gubbio in Umbria. Two small towns, Sigillo and Costacciaro, near Gubbio, sent many immigrants to the Iron Range.[3]

While the present state of research does not permit a precise description of this pattern, it is clear that we are dealing with a special kind of migration. These were experienced miners moving within the international labor market of the mining industry, responding to changing opportunities. A common pattern was to immigrate to the mines of Luxembourg, France, or Alsace-Lorraine, then to the coal fields of Pennsylvania, and from there to the Upper Peninsula, and finally to Minnesota.

Other important regional groups in northern Minnesota came from Piedmont, the Tyrol, Veneto, Abruzzi, Campania, and Calabria. Despite the relatively small population, there was a mix of Italians from the northern, central and southern regions, but in contrast to Italian settlements elsewhere in the United States, those coming from north of Rome predominated on the Iron Range. These regional groupings were reflected in patterns of settlement and community life. Northern and central Italians, for example, were predominant on the eastern end of the Mesabi, while the southerners tended to concentrate on the western end. Another distinction was that those from the north and central regions, because of their earlier date of arrival and prior mining experience, tended to have better-paying jobs. Attilio Castigliano,

---

[3]Castigliano, "Origine," pp. 733–39; Virtue, *Minnesota Iron Ranges*, p. 356; U.S. Immigration Commission, *Immigrants in Industries*, vol. 16, p. 330; Sulfur mines of Boratella Terza, Archivio di Stato, Forli, Prefettura di Forli, Archivio di Gabinetto, Affari riservate diversi, Busta 128, Anno 188, Fasc. 93; Emigration, Archivio Communale, Municipio di Sassoferrato; Padre Stefano Troiani, interview with author, Biblioteca Communale, Sassoferrato, 1 October 1981.

the Italian consular agent in Duluth, reported in 1913 that while the north and central Italians were employed in underground mines and regarded as excellent workers, the southerners were hired only for the lowest grades of work in the open-pit mines.[4]

Work on the Iron Range was hard and dangerous. The absolute power of the mining companies was personified by the mining captains and foremen. These bosses, usually Cornish or Scandinavian, mercilessly drove the new immigrants, toward whom they felt a "racial antagonism and superiority." Accidents were daily occurrences; between 1906 and 1909, 1 of every 200 miners was killed each year. Of the 292 fatalities during these years, 38 were Italians. Daily wages ranged from $2.50 for underground miners to $1.90 for surface laborers, and the cost of living was quite high. Opportunities for Italians to advance to supervisory or skilled jobs were few. Labor turnover was high; Teofilo Petriella, a labor organizer, observed that two-thirds of the men did not remain more than one or two years. Many Italians returned home from the Range bitterly disillusioned with America.[5]

The Italians played a significant, if at times equivocal, role in the history of the efforts to organize the Minnesota mines. For a half century, the Oliver Iron Mining Company refused to bargain collectively and used every means, including blacklisting and espionage, to frustrate organizing efforts. The first major attempt to challenge the power of the mining companies occurred in 1907. Petriella was appointed special organizer for the Mesabi Range by the Western Federation of Miners in June 1906. A native of Campania, a former school teacher, and a socialist, Petriella organized Finnish, "Austrian," and Italian branches of WFM locals on the Mesabi. The strike of 1907 was broken by the companies after several months through the use of "special deputies" and strikebreakers. Petriella, who had been attacked as an "alien Dago anarchist," left under a shadow, suspected of having appropriated strike funds.[6]

---

[4] Castigliano, "Origine," pp. 733–39; U.S. Immigration Commission, *Immigrants in Industries*, vol. 16, p. 340. Mining officials in Minnesota described the southern Italians as "inefficient and worthless ... fit but for the lowest grade of work in the open-pit mines."

[5] John Syrjamaki, "Mesabi Communities: A Study of their Development" (Ph.D. diss., Yale University, 1940), pp. 142, 188; Virtue, *Minnesota Iron Ranges*, pp. 367–76; U.S. Immigration Commission, *Immigrants in Industries*, vol. 16, pp. 318–23; 339; *The Miners Magazine* (Denver), 22 August 1907, p. 8.

[6] Hyman Berman, "Education for Work and Labor Solidarity: The Immigrant

Lincoln Mine crew, Virginia, 1912. Photo courtesy of Joseph Dellago.

Not until 1916 was there another big strike on the Range. Italian miner and agitator Joe Greeni touched off this revolt one day by walking off the job, taking the entire shift with him. Within a few days, all mining operations on the Mesabi were closed. The Industrial Workers of the World sent its best organizers to the Range, including Carlo Tresca. A native of Sulmona in the Abruzzi and an anarcho-syndicalist, Tresca became a prominent labor leader among Italian immigrants. During the Mesabi strike, two men were killed in a shooting fray. Although not at the scene, the IWW leaders, including Tresca, were arrested and indicted for murder. Tresca's arrest evoked a storm of protest in both the United States and Italy, and eventually he was released. Meanwhile, after four months of resistance, the strike ended in total defeat. Accounts of the strike and its aftermath by Efrem Bartoletti were published in *Il Proletario*, the Italian syndicalist organ. Bartoletti, a native of Costacciaro, was a miner and poet. His collected poems, which describe the life of the immigrant and miner, were published by the IWW under the title *Nostalgie proletarie*.[7]

It was not until the 1930s that a successful campaign by the Steel Workers' Organizing Committee of the CIO brought unionization to Minnesota's Iron Range. The Italians and South Slavs were most active in this organizing work. The director of SWOC, John T. Bernard, was born in Corsica of Italian parents. He was elected to the U.S. Congress in 1936 on the Farmer-Labor ticket. With the capitulation of the Oliver Iron Mining Company in 1943, the United Steel Workers

---

Miners and Radicalism on the Mesabi Range" (1963, ms. copy in Immigration History Research Center, University of Minnesota), pp. 38–45; Neil Betten, "Strike on the Mesabi—1907," *Minnesota History* 40 (Fall 1967): 340–47; Edward J. Marolt, "The Development of Labor Unionism in the Iron Mining Industry of the Virginia-Eveleth District" (M.A. thesis, University of Minnesota, 1969). On Petriella, see "Petriella, Teofilo," Casellario Politico Centrale, Ministero dell'Interno, Direzione Centrale di Pubblica Sicurezza, Archivio Centrale dello Stato (Rome); and "Report of Teofilo Petriella," Western Federation of Miners, *Proceedings of the Fifteenth Annual Convention, 1907* (Denver, 1907), pp. 185–90.

[7] Berman, "Education for Work and Labor Solidarity," pp. 46–55; Neil Betten, "Riot, Revolution, Repression in the Iron Range Strike of 1916," *Minnesota History* 41 (Summer 1968): 82–93; Donald G. Sofchalk, "Organized Labor and the Iron Ore Miners of Northern Minnesota, 1906–1936," *Labor History* 12 (Spring 1971): 214–42. On Tresca, see "Tresca, Carlo," Casellario Politico Centrale; and Arturo Caroti, *Per Carlo Tresca* (Milan, 1916). Bartoletti's poems and articles on the 1916 strike were published in *Il Proletario* (New York) 15 July 1916 and subsequent issues.

of America came to embrace every mine on the Range. Italian Americans have continued to provide a large percentage of the rank and file, as well as filling important leadership positions in the union.[8]

While the Italians settled in the towns, villages and mining locations along the full length of the eighty-mile Mesabi Range, they were most heavily concentrated in Hibbing, Eveleth, Chisholm, and Virginia. Many of the recent immigrants lived in the "locations" adjacent to the mines. Some had company housing, but others lived in shacks constructed of boards covered with tar paper. Since the Italians were predominantly male sojourners, they either boarded with a family or in a boardinghouse. As they were joined by women, permanent Italian communities emerged. Some small and isolated communities were entirely Italian or even entirely from a particular region, such as the Plymouth location outside of Chisholm. In larger towns such as Hibbing, there was a mix of regional groups. Here residential clustering by region was the rule: boarders tended to be *paesani*; marriages were arranged among *paesani*; and businesses operated by *paesani* were patronized. For quite some time, social life was compartmentalized along lines of *regionalismo* and *campanilismo*.[9]

The early leaders among the Italians on the Range were often saloon keepers who were in effect padrones. Usually former miners, they contracted with the mining companies for labor gangs, recruited workers and provided them with lodging, food, and drink, banked their money or sent it to Italy, and sold them steamship tickets. Petriella described this as a "form of slavery" in which the miners were kept by "their merchant and politician countrymen." As the Italian population grew, groceries, bakeries, barbershops, coal and ice dealers, and shoemakers, as well as saloons, proliferated. By the 1920s, one could also find doctors, lawyers, pharmacists, teachers, and nurses in the larger com-

---

[8] Rudolph Pinola, "Labor and Politics on the Iron Range of Northern Minnesota," (Ph.D. diss., University of Wisconsin, 1957), pp. 75–93; Paul H. Landis, *Three Iron Mining Towns: A Study in Cultural Change* (Ann Arbor, Mich., 1938), p. 111; Marolt, "Development of Labor Unionism," pp. 14–60. On Bernard, see Barbara Stuhler, "The One Man Who Voted 'Nay': The Story of John T. Bernard's Quarrel with American Foreign Policy, 1937–1939," *Minnesota History* 43 (Fall 1972): 90–92; and author's interview with Bernard, 11 September 1978.

[9] Syrjamaki, "Mesabi Communities," pp. 120, 126, 149; Castigliano, "Origine," p. 737; U.S. Immigration Commission, *Immigrants in Industries*, vol. 16, pp. 318–23, 348–50; Virtue, *Minnesota Iron Ranges*, pp. 356–59; Columbus Memorial Association of Minnesota, *Columbus: A Collection of Historical Facts* (St. Paul, 1931), pp. 70–78.

munities. A sociological study of the Iron Range in 1940, however, concluded that, compared with other ethnic groups, the Italians were somewhat slower to enter business and the professions.[10]

By the end of World War I, the Iron Range had ceased to attract new immigrants. Due to increased mechanization, ore production continued to increase while the size of the labor force declined. The impact of the depression was particularly severe in northern Minnesota. Some communities became ghost towns; in others, residents were dependent on municipal jobs and relief. As the exodus from the Iron Range continued, certain ethnic groups largely disappeared from the region, but the Italians remained in significant numbers. Many of the second generation left in search of greener pastures, but in time a goodly number returned. For the old-timers who had acquired property after a long struggle this was home; they were loathe to leave.[11]

An invidious distinction came to be made on the Iron Range between "white men," meaning northern Europeans, and the so-called "black races" of southern Europe. The English-speaking groups did not regard Italians as "white folk." These attitudes of superiority, which persisted at least until World War II, were exemplified by the march of hooded Klansmen through the Range cities and by the exclusion of southern Europeans from social and professional circles. Deep hostility existed between the "whites" and the "blacks." The tendency of the Italians to remain within their own group, while due in part to choice, was also a reaction to ostracism by the dominant Anglo-Scandinavian element. One consequence of this exclusion was that the Italians gradually came to recognize that their common identity as a nationality group was more important than regional differences and that only through unity could they challenge the entrenched WASPs.[12]

In their organizational life, for example, one can trace the trend toward greater cohesiveness. Initially, mutual aid societies were formed on the basis of regional and *paese* origins. In Hibbing, for example,

---

[10] Syrjamaki, "Mesabi Communities," pp. 129, 253; "Report of Teofilo Petriella," p. 190; Columbus Memorial Association, *Columbus*, pp. 70–78.

[11] Landis, *Three Iron Mining Towns*, p. 19; Syrjamaki, "Mesabi Communities," pp. 347–81; Adolfo Vinci, "Le miniere di ferro nel Minnesota," *Bollettino dell'emigrazione* no. 20 (Rome, 1923), pp. 16–20. Based also on extensive interviews conducted in the Range towns during the summer of 1981.

[12] Landis, *Three Iron Mining Towns*, p. 23; Syrjamaki, "Mesabi Communities," pp. 245–57, 378, 435; interviews.

the Tyrolese and the Piedmontese were the first to organize; they also maintained their societies on an exclusive regional basis the longest. In 1905, the *Società M.S. Guglielmo Marconi* was founded, and some years later the Cesare Cantù Lodge of the Order Sons of Italy in America was established. These merged in 1924 to form the Marconi Lodge, OSIA, whose impressive lodge hall became the center of Italian community activities. Such organizational mergers took place in other towns as well. The Italians in northern Minnesota also developed a common identity, a "Range consciousness." Following World War I, Italian Americanization Clubs, which were formed in towns and villages on the Range, merged into the Minnesota State Federation of Italian American Clubs. While the ostensible purpose was to promote naturalization, the federation's larger purpose was to mobilize the Italians politically. Reflecting their largely working-class character, the Range Italians tended to support the Farmer-Labor Party in the interwar years. Their strong political progressivism distinguished them from Italian Americans elsewhere. While their continuing struggle with the corporate power of the mining companies no doubt contributed to this militancy, one wonders to what extent the political culture of the immigrants from the "Red Zone" of Italy had an influence.[13]

Anticlericalism, for example, appears to have been widespread among the Italians on the Iron Range. The first Italian parish, the Church of the Immaculate Conception in Hibbing, was established in 1906. However, it was reported in 1909 that Italians there seldom went to church, often married in civil ceremonies, and did not baptize their children. Elsewhere on the Range, the Italians were either unchurched or belonged to ethnically mixed parishes. Viewing this as a promising field, the Presbyterian Home Board's Department of Immigration established a mission for the Italians in 1913. This initiated a "terrible struggle" between the Protestant missionaries and the Catholic church for the faith of the Italians. Presbyterian missionaries William J. Bell and Gaetano A. Lizzi initially made impressive gains with their tracts, portable organ, and stereopticon. Appealing to the Italians' anticlerical, nationalistic sentiments, Lizzi organized

---

[13] Columbus Memorial Association, *Columbus*, pp. 70–76; *Eveleth News-Clarion*, 31 July 1947; newspaper clippings, vertical file, Northeast Minnesota Historical Center, University of Minnesota, Duluth; records of the Guglielmo Marconi Lodge, Order Sons of Italy in America, Minnesota Historical Society.

the *Savonarola Circolo Educativo*. However, Bell's Iron Range parish appears to have made few permanent converts among the Italians. Its primary effect seems to have been to stimulate the Catholic church to provide churches and clergy for the neglected Italians. An Italian national parish, the Church of the Immaculate Conception, for example, was created in Eveleth in 1915. Of the Italian churches on the Iron Range, only the Church of the Immaculate Conception in Hibbing still exists, and it is no longer a national parish.[14]

There remains today a visible Italian presence on the Iron Range. Despite a general decline in the region's population, about one-fourth of Minnesota's Italian Americans still live there. Here as elsewhere the Italians have demonstrated a tenacious attachment to place; they have come to terms with the harsh environment and feel a strong love for this north country. After several generations the Italian Americans on the Range have made it. In business and the professions, they are perhaps the dominant element in the larger Range cities. And since World War II, Italian Americans have been elected mayor of cities such as Hibbing and Virginia, which had been strongholds of the "whites." The old mutual aid societies are defunct, but there are Italian American Clubs in many towns. The clubs, composed now for the most part of the second and third generations, are primarily social organizations. Their ethnic activities appear limited to sponsoring Columbus Day observances and an annual Range-wide *bocce* tournament.

Minnesota's Iron Range attracted an exotic mixture of ethnic groups; from this mix has emerged a Range culture that is a blend of many cultural ingredients. It includes the Finnish sauna, Slovenian *potica*, the Cornish pasty, and Italian *bocce*. *Bocce* is played by persons of all ethnic backgrounds; there are women's as well as men's leagues, and *bocce* courts are maintained and lighted by the municipalities. When Rudy Perpich, son of a Croatian miner, became

---

[14]Syrjamaki, "Mesabi Communities," p. 312; Giovanni Schiavo, *Italian American History* (New York, 1949), vol. 2, pp. 683–94; U.S. Work Projects Administration, "Minnesota Historical Records Survey: Churches, 1936–41," Minnesota Historical Society; Giovanni Zarrilli Papers, Diocese of Duluth Archives, College of St. Scholastica, Duluth; William J. Bell Papers, Minnesota Historical Society. On Bell see also Clarke A. Chambers, "Social Welfare Policies and Programs on the Minnesota Iron Range—1800–1930" (1963, ms. copy in Immigration History Research Center, University of Minnesota), pp. 65–76.

governor, one of his objectives was to establish a *bocce* court in every town in Minnesota.[15]

From the common experiences of mining and adapting to an austere environment, the children and grandchildren of the immigrants, Finns, Slovenes, Swedes, Italians, and others, fashioned a shared "Iron Ranger" identity. Despite a powerful sense of community, however, the young have been leaving the Range for decades. A region dominated by one industry, the Range has been particularly vulnerable to the vagaries of capitalism. The Rangers' destinies have from the beginning been determined in the corporate boardrooms of Pittsburgh, Cleveland, and New York. A boom that brought jobs and new hope to northern Minnesota with the introduction of the taconite process of ore extraction in the 1960s had collapsed by the 1980s. In the face of cheaper imported steel and iron ore, mining operations on the Range closed down. Once again economic depression devastated the region, and once again people picked up and left in search of work elsewhere. Ironically, the grandchildren of the immigrants who had been drawn to northern Minnesota by jobs in the mines were now forced to become migrants themselves. Italian Americans, of course, were as subject to these forces as others. Still, their communities displayed impressive resilience in surviving previous crises, and I would wager that the colorful and turbulent history of the Italians on the Iron Range is not at an end.

---

[15] Newspaper clippings, Northeast Minnesota Historical Center; Newspaper clippings, John A. Vannelli Papers, Immigration History Research Center, University of Minnesota; Elizabeth Mathias, "Summary of Findings of Italian American Culture on the Iron Range," (1978, ms. in Iron Range Historical Society, Gilbert, Minn.).

About the Authors

JOHN ANDREOZZI is coordinator of the Sons of Italy Archives Project at the Immigration History Research Center, University of Minnesota. His M.A. thesis, for the University of Wisconsin, Milwaukee, traced the assimilation of Milwaukee's Italians. Andreozzi is preparing a book on the Italian experience in Lackawanna, New York.

VALENTINE J. BELFIGLIO is associate professor of government at Texas Women's University. He is author of *The Italian Experience in Texas*, for which he was awarded the Guido Dorso Prize in Literature in the category of research. Belfiglio received his Ph.D. from the University of Oklahoma.

CARLA BIANCO is professor of ethnology at the University of Florence and author of *The Two Rosetos*. She received her Ph.D. in folklore studies at Indiana University.

PHYLIS CANCILLA MARTINELLI teaches sociology at Arizona State University. She has done extensive research on the Italian American communities in San Francisco and Phoenix. Her Ph.D. dissertation, on contemporary Italian American migrants to Scottsdale, Arizona, will be published soon by AMS Press.

ERNESTO MILANI received a degree in modern languages from the

192 About the Authors

University of Milan with a thesis on mutual aid societies among Italian immigrants in the United States. As an "ethnic archaeologist," Milani has organized several photographic exhibits on Italian emigration to North America, and is now working on a micro-analysis of Italian settlements in the United States and Canada.

JACQUELINE ROCCHIO MORAN is employed at Glensheen Museum, Duluth. She received an M.A. in history from the University of Minnesota, Duluth.

JOHN POTESTIO teaches history at Lakeview High School, Thunder Bay. He received an M.A. in history from Lakehead University, and is author of *The History of the Italian Mutual Benefit Society, 1929–1985*. Potestio has written a number of articles on Giovanni Veltri and the R.F. Welch Company of Thunder Bay.

ANTONIO PUCCI is a history instructor with the Lakehead District Catholic School Board. He received an M.A. in history from Lakehead University and has written extensively on Italian immigration and the Italian community of Thunder Bay. Pucci is currently co-editing a volume on the Italian immigrant experience in North America.

RYAN RUDNICKI is an assistant professor in the Department of Geography and Planning, Southwest Texas State University. He received a Ph.D. in geography, with a concentration in population, from Pennsylvania State University. He is currently working with computer applications in geography and demographics.

PAOLA A. SENSI-ISOLANI is associate professor of anthropology and modern languages at St. Mary's College of California. She received a Ph.D. in anthropology from the University of California, Berkeley.

PAUL A. STURGUL is a practicing attorney and local historian in Hurley, Wisconsin. He is a graduate of the University of Wisconsin, Madison.

RUDOLPH J. VECOLI is professor of history at the University of Minnesota and director of the University's Immigration History Research Center. His most recent essay is "The Search for an Italian American Identity: Continuity and Change," in *Italian Americans*, Lydio Tomasi, ed. (New York, 1985).

JOHN ZUCCHI is assistant professor of history at McGill University, Montreal. He received his Ph.D. from the University of Toronto, with a dissertation on the Italians of Toronto. He has authored several articles on Italian immigrants.

Italian Immigrants in Rural and Small Town America

AIHA Fourteenth Annual Conference, 1981

FRIDAY, OCTOBER 30

8:30 a.m.
F.K. Wyerhaeuser
Auditorium

Registration, Coffee

9:00
Auditorium

Welcome
George Latimer, Mayor of St. Paul

9:15-10:30
Auditorium

Immigrant Folk Cultures: Processes of Acculturation and Problems of Documentation

Chair: *Rudolph J. Vecoli, University of Minnesota*

Carla Bianco, Università degli Studi di Firenze

10:45

Concurrent Sessions

Auditorium

Session A: Italians in the Lake Superior Region

Chair: *Joseph A. Amato, Southwest Minnesota State University*

Jacqueline Rocchio Moran, Duluth, Minnesota
"Duluth's 'Little Italies' "

Antonio Pucci, Multicultural Association of Thunder Bay
"Two 'Little Italies' at the Head of the Lakes"

John Potestio, Multicultural Association of Thunder Bay
"Itinerant *Grimaldesi: Paesani* on the Railways of North America"

Rudolph J. Vecoli, University of Minnesota
"Italians on Minnesota's Iron Ranges"

Room 317

Session B: Italians in Mining Communities

Chair: *Ernest Rossi, Western Michigan University*

Phylis Cancilla Martinelli, Arizona State University
"Piedmontese Pioneers in Globe, Arizona"

Greta Swenson, Northland College, Ashland, Wisconsin
"Italians in Hurley-Ironwood"

Paul Sturgul, Hurley, Wisconsin
"Italians on the Gogebic Range"

12:30 p.m.
Cortile

Lunch

1:30-3:15	*Concurrent Sessions*
Auditorium	**Session A: Italians in Canada (Joint Session of Canadian Italian Historical Association)**

Chair: *Bruno Ramirez, University of Montreal*

John Zucchi, University of Toronto
"Friulani Networks in North America"

Franc Sturino, Ontario Institute for Studies in Education
"Calabrese Truck Farmers on the Outskirts of a Metropolis"

Angelo Principe, University of Toronto
"The Genovese Precursors of Toronto's 'Little Italy,'
1840-1870"

Comment: *Robert Perrin, York University*

Room 317   **Session B: Settlement Patterns, Ethnicity, and Assimilation in Rural America**

Chair: *William M. DeMarco, Harvard University*

Paolo A. Sensi-Isolani, St. Mary's College of California
"Tradition and Transition: Italians in a Northern California *paese"*

Kristin Ruggiero, Indiana University
"Assimilation Among Italo-Argentine Farmers"

Francis X. Femminella, State University of New York-Albany
"Rural-Urban Contrasts in Identity Elements of Rural Italian Americans"

Ryan Rudnicki, State University of New York-Oneonta
"Italian Immigrant Settlements in Rural/Small Town America"

3:30-5:00 p.m.   *Concurrent Sessions*

Room 317   **Session A: Italians in Texas**

Chair: *George E. Pozzetta, University of Florida*

Dino Cinel, Tulane University, New Orleans
"Italians in Peonage"

Valentino J. Belfiglio, Texas Woman's University
"Texas Immigrants from the Mezzogiorno, 1870-1914"

Harral E. Landry, Texas Woman's University
"Italians and Texas Culture"

Auditorium   **Session B: Italians in West Virginia Coal Mining**

Chair: *Philip F. Notarianni, Utah State Historical Society*

Dianne Francesconi Lyon, Silver Spring, Maryland
"Italians in West Virginia Mining Communities"

Randall G. Lawrence, West Virginia Coal Life Project
"Italians in Appalachia, 1880-1914"

Joseph L. Tropea, George Washington University
" *Sotto La Terra: Tutti Morti*: West Virginia Mine Disaster of 1907"

6:30   **Reception: Venetian Inn, 2814 Rice St., St. Paul** *(Bus transportation will be provided.)*

7:30   **Dinner**

Speaker: *Bruce F. Vento, U.S. Congressman*

Entertainment: Medley of Italian Songs
                Jo Ann Piccolo, Vocalist
                Rosie Mayer, Accompanist

                Selections of Italian Dances
                I Ballerini Italiani di Minnesota

SATURDAY, OCTOBER 31

8:30 a.m.   **Registration, Coffee**
Auditorium

8:30   **AIHA Annual Business Meeting**
Room 408

9:30-11:15   *Concurrent Sessions*

Auditorium   **Session A: Italians in the Midwest**

Chair: *Nina M. Archabal, Minnesota Historical Society*

Thomas M. Shaw, University of Northern Iowa
"Oelwein, Iowa: An Italian Railroad Settlement"

John Andreozzi, Milwaukee
"Cumberland, Wisconsin: From the Dillingham
Commission to the Present"

Dorothy Schwieder, Iowa State University
"Italian Americans in Iowa's Coal Mining Industry"

Room 317   **Session B: Italians in the Deep South**

Chair: *Gary Mormino, University of South Florida*

Julia M.L. Scarano, Universidade Estadual Paulista
"*Julio de Mesquita Filho*," Sao Paulo, Brazil
"Italians in a Coffee Country"

Paul Giordano, Rosary College, River Forest, Illinois
"Italians and the Strawberry Industry in Tangipahoa Parish,
Louisiana"

Ernesto R. Milani, Gallarte, Italy
"*Marchigiani* and *Veneti* in Sunnyside Plantation,
Arkansas"

Louis Guida, Little Rock, Arkansas
"The Sunnyside Plantation Revisited: What Has Happened
Since 1895?"

11:30   *Concurrent Sessions*

Auditorium   **Session A: Italian Immigrants and the American Land**

Chair: *Jay P. Dolan, University of Notre Dame*

Gianfausto Rosoli, Centro Studi Emigrazione, Rome
"Agricultural Colonization Projects in the United States
and Italian Government Policy"

Robert Viscusi, Brooklyn College
"The Text in the Dust: Writing Italy Across America"

Frank J. Cavaioli, *State University of New York-Farmingdale*
"Charles Angelo Siringo, Italian American Cowboy"

Room 317   **Session B: The Other New York Italians**

Chair: *Lydio Tomasi, Center for Migration Studies*

Helen Barolini, *Ossining, New York*
"An Italian Hill-Town on the Hudson: Dobbs Ferry, New York"

David P. Starna, *Oswego, New York*
"Migration Networks in Upstate New York: Seneca Falls"

Michael A. LaSorte, *State University of New York-Brockport*
"Italians in Upstate New York, 1900: A Census Analysis"

1:00 p.m.   **Lunch**
Cortile

2:00-4:00   **Films**
Auditorium

Charles A. Jarvis, *Dickinson College* presents *Amerigo, Mascita di una Canzone*

Antonello Branca, *Radio-Televisione-Italiana, Rome* presents *A.P. Giannini and the Bank of America*

4:30-6:30   **Reception and Open House**
Immigration
History Research
Center

Conference Committee

Lynn Toscano, former president, Stella del Nord Chapter, AIHA

Program: Rudolph J. Vecoli

Local Arrangements: Dolores Colangelo, Fred Ventura

Publicity: Dominic Arbisi, James Zappa

Administration: Dominic Greco

Entertainment: Catherine Piccolo

Financial contributions in support of the conference are acknowledged from the following:

Columbus Memorial Association

Italian American Club of Duluth and the Women's Auxiliary

Italian American Progressive Club of Hibbing

St. Paul Chapter of UNICO National

Jeno's Inc.

A special thanks to all the volunteers who contributed their time to this conference.

Index